ESSENTIAL CHEMISTRY

THE PERIODIC TABLE

ESSENTIAL CHEMISTRY

Atoms, Molecules, and Compounds

Chemical Reactions

Metals

The Periodic Table

States of Matter

ESSENTIAL CHEMISTRY

THE PERIODIC TABLE

BECKY HAM

CHELSEA HOUSE
PUBLISHERS
An imprint of Infobase Publishing

THE PERIODIC TABLE

Chelsea House
An imprint of Infobase Publishing
132 West 31st Street
New York NY 10001

Library of Congress Cataloging-in-Publication Data
Ham, Becky.
  The Periodic table / Becky Ham.
    p. cm. — (Essential chemistry)
  Includes bibliographical references and index.
  ISBN-13: 978-0-7910-9533-1 (hardcover)
  ISBN-10: 0-7910-9533-9 (hardcover)
  1. Periodic law—Tables. 2. Chemical elements. I. Title. II. Series.

  QD467.H335 2007
  546'.8—dc22   2007022400

Text design by Erik Lindstrom
Cover design by Ben Peterson

Printed in the United States of America

Bang NMSG 10 9 8 7 6 5 4 3 2 1

CONTENTS

What Is the Periodic Table?

In 1977, two space probes lifted off from Earth on a mission to the outer reaches of the solar system. Voyager 1 and 2 each carried a unique item among the usual scientific instruments: a golden record filled with pictures, sounds, songs, and languages from around the world. The record was made of gold wrapped around a disc of copper, since recordings made on metal plates last longer and remain clearer than recordings made on ordinary plastic. The record, packaged with a needle and a power source to act as a basic record player, was designed to last for millions of years in outer space.

The golden record was meant to be a quick guide to the Earth for anyone or anything that came across Voyager 1 or 2 during their journeys across the stars. The pictures on the record were supposed to show what kinds of plants and animals lived on Earth, what the Earth itself looked like and what humans were like at all ages and in all countries. Other images included snowflakes, houses, an X-ray of a hand, diagrams of a woman giving birth, crocodiles, and even an astronaut in space. The golden record also included "greetings from Earth" in 55 different languages, 90 minutes of music from around the world, and noises such as the sound of a chirping cricket, the wind in a storm, and laughter. The cover of the golden record was marked with simple math symbols and drawings that explained what the record was and how it should be played.

Although it did not make it onto the golden record, there is one picture that could have explained all the materials that make up the people, animals, plants, rocks, oceans, and the rest of Earth. That picture is the **periodic table of the elements**.

The periodic table answers the question "what are things made of?" If it sounds like something a small child might ask, it is good to remember that the answer was not obvious for thousands of years of human history. Before the question was answered, the periodic table did not exist, even in the imaginations of the most thoughtful scientists.

Today, we know that things are made of elements. An **element** is a basic building block of matter. **Matter** is the material that makes up everything in the universe, from stars to spacecraft to golden records. The periodic table is a list of all the basic building blocks of matter that are found naturally, along with some building blocks that have been created in the laboratory here on Earth.

THE BASICS OF EVERYTHING

Most matter is a combination of materials, just as the matter of an astronaut is a combination of skin, hair, bones, muscles, and even the cloth, plastic, rubber, and metal in his or her spacesuit. Something like "skin" is not a basic building block of matter, because it can be broken down into smaller building blocks, cells. Cells are made up of even smaller building blocks—water—which is in turn made up of even smaller building blocks: elements called *oxygen* and *hydrogen*.

Figure 1.1   Chicago boasted the world's largest exhibition of the periodic table of the elements with this display on the exterior of the Richard J. Daley Center.

Oxygen and hydrogen are elements because they are the smallest blocks of a certain kind of matter. Oxygen cannot be broken down into anything else. Hydrogen cannot be broken down into anything else. If a piece of matter cannot be broken down into more than one type of matter, it is an element.

The periodic table is more than just a list of elements. After all, a list could take any shape. The periodic table takes its shape from the way elements are related to each other. The shape of the table can predict what a certain element might look like, even if it has never been seen before. The shape of the periodic table can be used to tell which elements will react with others. The shape of the periodic table can even be used to picture the smallest particles of an element, particles far smaller than anything the human eye or even most microscopes could ever see.

The modern periodic table first appeared as a page for a chemistry textbook, written by a teacher who thought his students needed an easy way to look at the elements. The shape of the table made it world-famous, for all the reasons mentioned. The carefully stacked rows and columns made a simple list into a useful tool and a snapshot of how matter is organized on Earth and throughout the universe.

SUMMARY

The periodic table is a chart that includes all of the natural and artificial elements known in the universe. Elements are basic building blocks of matter. The periodic table is more than a list of the elements. It is also a guide and tool to understanding all chemical reactions and the materials involved in building the Earth and the universe. This book will describe the history and science behind the periodic table and take an in-depth look at all the major groups of elements.

The History of the Periodic Table

The idea of an element as a basic type of material, different from other materials, has been around for at least 2 million years, when the first people to make stone tools appeared on the scene. These early humans chose different types of rock for different tools, knowing that certain kinds of rock were more likely to break into small flakes or keep their sharp edge. Although they probably did not think about the "building blocks" of the rocks themselves, they knew that the material of some rocks was different from the material of other rocks.

The idea of building blocks grew when people began changing materials in more complicated ways, such as baking wheat into bread or melting metal into weapons. These ancient chemists chose materials not just because they were useful on their own, but also because they were useful and sometimes very different when they were combined with other materials.

Thousands of years ago, people knew about elements such as tin, copper, gold, silver, and even mercury, but they did not think of them as basic building blocks. Ancient Greek scholars thought that the real elements of the world were opposites such as "hot," "cold," "wet," and "dry"—or materials such as fire, earth, air, and water that were made by combining these opposites. In China, philosophers recognized five *xing*, or phases of fire, earth, water, wood, and metal. The Greek philosopher Aristotle (384–322 B.C.) thought a material like gold could be built by combining elements, such as fire and earth, in the right pattern.

There was one early hint at the modern way of thinking of elements, from the ancient Greek scholar Democritus (~460–~370 B.C.), who thought that materials like fire were made up of tiny invisible particles that could not be broken into smaller pieces. The word he used for these particles is *atomos*. **Atoms**, as they are called today, are the particles that make up elements. The element gold is made up of gold atoms; the element lead is made of lead atoms, and so on.

Aristotle's idea that the four ancient elements could be mixed into any kind of material sparked a centuries-long interest in **alchemy**. Part scientists and part philosophers, alchemists looked for ways to change plain metals, such as lead, into more valuable metals, like gold. If Aristotle was right, the two metals were simply different arrangements of the same four elements. The alchemists searched for a method to change these elements' arrangement in lead into their arrangement in gold.

Some alchemists were little more than con men who tried to convince others that they could do things like make gold out of thin air or cure any disease with a pure potion they called *acqua vitae*. Many alchemists worked like scientists, testing different ideas about matter with careful experiments. Their studies paved the way for the first true chemists and the modern definition of an element.

MODERN ELEMENTS, MODERN CHEMISTRY

In the late seventeenth and early eighteenth centuries, alchemists began to doubt the idea that there were only four main elements. Their laboratory experiments uncovered a variety of strange materials that did not seem to fit the ancient pattern. For instance, alchemists discovered that they could produce "airs" or **gases** in their laboratories by burning different kinds of materials like wood and metals. According to the ancient classification, all of these gases should be the same element, but they acted differently when they were themselves burned.

In laboratories around Europe, alchemists were also "creating"—discovering, really—new elements such as phosphorus in their quest for gold. Phosphorus, which German alchemists first produced by boiling human urine, glowed brilliantly as if it were on fire without producing any smoke or fumes. As alchemists worked to figure out the secrets of phosphorus and other odd concoctions, and voyages to the New World turned up strange new metals such as platinum, Europeans began to realize there might be a wide variety of basic building blocks.

The idea of the atom also made a comeback in the late seventeenth century, thanks in part to Scottish alchemist Robert Boyle (1627–1691). Boyle thought that all matter must be made of atoms that come in different shapes and sizes, like toy blocks. He suggested that materials like gold and lead are both made of atoms, but the size and shape of the atoms are different in gold and lead.

Boyle was both an alchemist and chemist, but the researchers who followed him left alchemy behind as they pursued the new science of chemistry. Their experiments, which were now carefully written down and repeated, revealed new metals, like cobalt and nickel, and new gases, such as nitrogen and oxygen. In 1789, the French chemist Antoine Laurent de Lavoisier (1743–1794) offered the first modern definition of an element: a chemical substance

Figure 2.1
John Dalton surmised that each element is made of atoms specific to that element. This theory led to the modern understanding of atomic mass: Each element has a different mass because of its unique atomic composition.

that could not be broken down into another substance. Lavoisier named more than 30 elements himself, before his head was cut off by the guillotine during the French Revolution. Although he was a brilliant scientist, Lavoisier also worked as a tax collector for the government and was a member of the aristocratic class, which made him unpopular with the revolutionaries.

John Dalton (1766–1844), a science teacher in England, combined the idea of the atom and Lavoisier's new definition of elements. He suggested that there were different kinds of atoms behind different elements. In this case, gold was built out of gold atoms, and lead was built out of lead atoms. Dalton also figured out a way to estimate the weight of each kind of atom. Other chemists had noticed that elements always combined together in a certain way. For instance, hydrogen always made up 15% of the weight of water, whereas oxygen accounted for 85% of water's weight. Using these numbers, Dalton figured out how much a hydrogen atom and an oxygen atom weigh. Scientists began to organize the growing list of elements with the help of these **atomic weights**.

TURNING LISTS INTO TABLES

The list of elements grew throughout the eighteenth and early nineteenth centuries, but it remained just a list. Eventually, chemists started to recognize little patterns within the list. The researchers used better estimates of atomic weight to arrange the list in order from lightest to heaviest element. Some chemists focused on elements that formed a "triad," or group of three, where the three elements had similar chemical properties and the weight of the middle element was the average of the lightest and heaviest elements in the triad. Others chemists saw a repeating pattern of eight chemically similar elements, where the lightest or first element was similar to the eighth-heaviest element, the second lightest element was similar to the ninth-heaviest element, and so on. Other scientists broke the list into groups of elements that acted in similar ways when they were part of a chemical **reaction**.

Although these patterns helped chemists organize the list of elements, the researchers thought the new groups were mostly just helpful tools. When a new element was discovered that did not fit the pattern, the chemists sometimes ignored the pattern and stuck the new element into the list where they thought it should fit based on its weight. Some chemists said the pattern only applied to some elements and not others. Most of the researchers thought the triads and the groups of eight did describe similar elements, but they were not sure whether these groups offered any clues as to *why* these elements were similar.

Figure 2.2   Dmitri Mendeleyev, a Russian chemistry teacher, devised the periodic table as a reference for his chemistry students. His work provided the foundation for today's periodic table.

MENDELEYEV'S TEXTBOOK TABLE

The periodic table finally made its debut in 1869, on a cold and stormy day in Petersburg, Russia. Chemistry teacher Dmitri Mendeleyev was writing a new textbook for his students when he hit upon the answer to a problem about elements that he had been thinking about for a while.

In the textbook, Mendeleyev wrote about groups of elements that looked alike and acted similarly in reactions, such as lithium, sodium, and potassium. As he wrote about the groups, the teacher thought it would be helpful to have some simple way of organizing all the elements to show these similarities.

Mendeleyev had collected a lot of information about the known elements, such as their atomic weights, their roles in chemical reactions and their melting temperatures. Some researchers say Mendeleyev dreamed up some version of the periodic table during an afternoon nap. Other historians say Mendeleyev made up separate cards for each element, with their details jotted on them like baseball cards. He then sorted the cards over and over in different ways until he came up with the pattern that became the periodic table.

Like others before him, Mendeleyev noticed a repeating pattern among the 63 known elements when they were listed in order of atomic weight. The pattern was **periodic**, meaning that the pattern repeated itself after a certain number of elements. In Mendeleyev's first periodic table, the pattern repeated with every seventh element, with the exception of the first element hydrogen. For instance, lithium was similar to sodium, which appeared seven elements after it in the table. Potassium, which was similar to sodium and lithium, appeared seven elements after sodium. In today's periodic table, lithium, sodium and potassium sit on top of each other in a column. Mendeleyev first arranged the table so that these similar elements would form a horizontal line, but later turned the table so that it looked more like the modern version.

— 70 —

но въ ней, мнѣ кажется, уже ясно выражается примѣнимость вы ставляемаго мною начала ко всей совокупности элементовъ, пай которыхъ извѣстенъ съ достовѣрностію. На этотъ разъ я и желалъ преимущественно найдти общую систему элементовъ. Вотъ этотъ опытъ:

			Ti=50	Zr=90	?=180.
			V=51	Nb=94	Ta=182.
			Cr=52	Mo=96	W=186.
			Mn=55	Rh=104,4	Pt=197,4
			Fe=56	Ru=104,4	Ir=198.
		Ni=Co=59	Pl=106,6	Os=199.
H=1			Cu=63,4	Ag=108	Hg=200.
	Be=9,4	Mg=24	Zn=65,2	Cd=112	
	B=11	Al=27,4	?=68	Ur=116	Au=197?
	C=12	Si=28	?=70	Sn=118	
	N=14	P=31	As=75	Sb=122	Bi=210
	O=16	S=32	Se=79,4	Te=128?	
	F=19	Cl=35,5	Br=80	I=127	
Li=7	Na=23	K=39	Rb=85,4	Cs=133	Tl=204
		Ca=40	Sr=57,6	Ba=137	Pb=207.
		?=45	Ce=92		
		?Er=56	La=94		
		?Yt=60	Di=95		
		?In=75,6	Th=118?		

а потому приходится въ разныхъ рядахъ имѣть различное измѣненіе разностей, чего нѣтъ въ главныхъ числахъ предлагаемой таблицы. Или же придется предполагать при составленіи системы очень много недостающихъ членовъ. То и другое мало выгодно. Мнѣ кажется притомъ, наиболѣе естественнымъ составить кубическую систему (предлагаемая есть плоскостная), но и попытки для ея образованія не повели къ надлежащимъ результатамъ. Слѣдующія двѣ попытки могутъ показать то разнообразіе сопоставленій, какое возможно при допущеніи основнаго начала, высказаннаго въ этой статьѣ.

Li	Na	K	Cu	Rb	Ag	Cs	—	Tl
7	23	39	63,4	85,4	108	133		204
Be	Mg	Ca	Zn	Sr	Cd	Ba	—	Pb
B	Al	—	—	—	Ur	—	—	Bi?
C	Si	Ti	—	Zr	Sn	—	—	—
N	P	V	As	Nb	Sb	—	Ta	—
O	S	—	Se	—	Te	—	W	—
F	Cl	—	Br	—	J	—	—	—
19	35,5	58	80	190	127	160	190	220.

Figure 2.3   Mendeleyev first organized his table so that the elements were situated vertically by atomic mass and horizontally according to their physical and chemical properties. Mendeleyev left spaces within his table, sensing that there were other elemental pieces of the puzzle to be discovered.

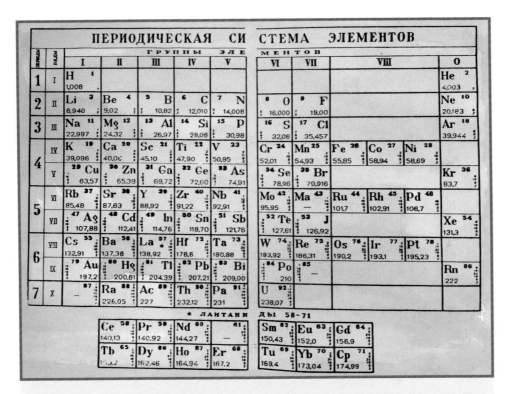

Figure 2.4   This version of Mendeleyev's periodic table was published in 1925. The elements have been rearranged from Mendeleyev's original list into a more accessible and better-structured model.

THE POWER OF PREDICTION

Mendeleyev's periodic table became the one of the most famous diagrams in the history of science—but why? After all, many other scientists had come up with their own ways of organizing the elements. In fact, a German chemist named Lothar Meyer created a periodic table just a few months before Mendeleyev wrote his table. What was it about Mendeleyev's table that made it so special?

Surprisingly, Mendeleyev's table became the periodic table used today because he left part of it blank. He put question marks in spaces where he thought there *should* be an element of a certain

MENDELEYEV AND THE GHOSTS

In November 1875, Dmitri Mendeleyev lit a match for a few seconds in a dark room in Petersburg, Russia. The brief flare startled the other people gathered around a table in the dark with Mendeleyev, including two young English brothers who said they could speak with ghosts. A few minutes later, one of the brothers fell to the floor in a fit, the lights went back on, and the arguments began.

The English brothers and the lit match were all part of a scientific investigation of séances—gatherings where people called mediums claimed to contact spirits of the dead. Séances were part of a movement called Spiritualism that became popular in the United States and Russia in the late nineteenth century.

Mendeleyev distrusted the Spiritualists because he thought they encouraged superstitious rather than scientific thought. He worried that the noble families who ran the government of the Russian Empire would ignore the advice of scientists and listen instead to the Spiritualists. Mendeleyev was also convinced that many mediums were fakes.

Mendeleyev led a scientific investigation of séances in 1875, hoping to prove to Russians that Spiritualism was mostly "dreams and hallucinations." Mendeleyev's lit match caught the English mediums as they attempted to ring a bell behind a curtain and blame the noise on spirits.

The interrupted séance and others like it convinced the scientists that the ghosts summoned by Spiritualism were fakes. Although Mendeleyev became something of a Russian celebrity after many speeches against Spiritualism, his countrymen remained fascinated by the spirit world for years after his investigation.

atomic weight, even though no element of that weight had been discovered yet. He even predicted what those missing elements would look like, based on the pattern he had figured out for the table.

He left blank spaces below boron, aluminum, and silicon, but he predicted that elements would be found for each of these spaces.

NAME THAT ELEMENT

The discoverers of gallium, scandium, and germanium proudly named their new elements after their home countries. Gallium comes from *Gallia*, the Latin name for France. Scandium was named for Scandinavia, whereas germanium was named after Germany. How did all the other elements get their names?

Some elements such as gold and silver have simple names, but are known by their Latin abbreviations in the periodic table. The symbol for gold—Au—comes from *aurum*, the Latin word for gold. The Latin word for silver is *argentum*, which explains why its symbol in the table is Ag.

Many of the newest elements discovered or created in the laboratory during the twentieth century are named after famous scientists. For instance, there is element 101, mendelevium. Does that name sound familiar?

Today, scientists who discover a new element must have the new name and symbol approved by the International Union of Pure and Applied Chemistry. (This book uses the official IUPAC periodic table.) IUPAC suggests that scientists name new elements after "a mythological concept, a mineral, a place or country, a property or a scientist." Before the new name becomes official, scientists can call the element by its atomic number. For instance, roentgenium was once named simply "element 111" or "ununbium," which is the Latin word for 111.

He predicted their atomic weights and other features such as their melting and boiling points. He even predicted how they would react with other common elements like oxygen.

The first blank was filled in 1875. A French chemist discovered an element—gallium—that had all the properties Mendeleyev predicted for the space below aluminum. In 1879, a Swedish researcher discovered scandium, which looked and acted exactly how Mendeleyev said it would in its place below boron. In 1886, a German scientist discovered germanium, the element below silicon. Its chemical properties were almost exactly what Mendeleyev had predicted.

The three discoveries helped make Mendeleyev's table more than just a clever way of arranging the elements. His amazingly accurate predictions about the new elements made it clear to other scientists that his table was something more than a fancy list. It was a powerful tool that could be used to hunt down new elements. It was a **hypothesis**, a scientific statement about the world that researchers could use to test other questions in chemistry.

Mendeleyev is famous today as the father of the periodic table because he was the first to recognize that the elements followed a pattern in real life, not just in chemists' notebooks. He did not make the periodic table of elements; he *discovered* it. The pattern already existed in nature; now it was up to Mendeleyev and others to figure out where elements belonged in the pattern.

SUMMARY

Ancient cultures thought there were only a handful of elements that made up all the matter in the world. The idea that these few elements could be mixed into any material led to the development of alchemy. Part scientists and part philosophers, alchemists searched for a way to turn common metal into gold. Their experiments paved the way for true chemists' research in the seventeenth and eighteenth centuries. Experiments by Robert Boyle, Antoine Laurent de Lavoisier, John Dalton, and others led to new definitions of an element. Later classifications of elements eventually led to the modern periodic table created by Dmitri Mendeleyev. Mendeleyev's table became a success when he correctly predicted new element discoveries.

What Elements Are Made of

One of the strangest things about Mendeleyev's discovery of the periodic table is that he did not really know why the table was periodic. He did not understand what elements really are in the way that scientists understand them now. Yet he was able to write out a correct periodic table that allowed him to make amazing predictions about unknown elements. He found an idea that worked, but he did not know *why* it worked.

Today, we know that elements fit into a periodic pattern because they are made of atoms, just as Democritus suspected. An atom is the smallest particle of an element that still has all the properties of that element. In other words, an atom of gold is no different from a bar of gold except that the atom is much smaller.

Democritus was wrong when he said that atoms could not be divided into smaller pieces. Atoms themselves are made of three smaller particles: the **proton**, the **neutron,** and the **electron**. Protons have a positive electrical charge, electrons have a negative electrical charge, and neutrons have no charge at all. Usually, an atom has the same number of protons and electrons. The positive and negative electrical charges of these two types of particles cancel each other out, such that an atom has no overall charge. Some atoms do have an overall positive or negative electrical charge, because they have an extra electron or are missing an electron. These charged atoms are called **ions**.

Protons and neutrons clump together to form the center of an atom, called the **nucleus.** The positive electrical charge of the protons attracts the negatively charged electrons in the same way the opposite poles of a magnet pull toward each other. This pull holds the electrons around the nucleus as if they were planets orbiting a sun, although the paths they take around the nucleus are not as steady or predictable as a planet's orbit. Instead, electrons move around the nucleus through wide spaces called **electron shells** that wrap around the nucleus like the layers of an onion.

An element can be defined by the number of protons in its atoms. All hydrogen atoms have only one proton, whereas all iron atoms have 26 protons and all gold atoms have 47 protons. The number of neutrons can vary, and there are usually more neutrons than protons in elements heavier than aluminum. Atoms of the same element that have different atomic weights due to different numbers of neutrons in the nucleus are called **isotopes**. Most of the weight of an atom comes from its protons and neutrons. Protons and neutrons have nearly the same **mass**, or to put it another way, they contain nearly the same amounts of matter. A proton has almost 2,000 times more mass than an electron.

When Mendeleyev first arranged his periodic table, he put the known elements in order of atomic weight. In the modern table, elements are arranged instead by **atomic number**—the number of protons they contain. The atomic number and the atomic weight are different because atomic weight also includes the contribution of electrons and neutrons. Luckily for Mendeleyev, the elements fall into roughly the same order whether they are ranked by atomic number or atomic weight.

WHY THE PERIODIC TABLE IS PERIODIC

Mendeleyev did not think elements were made of atoms, although many of his fellow chemists had already accepted the fact that atoms were the particles that made up all matter. In any case, no one in Mendeleyev's time even guessed at the fact that atoms were made of even smaller particles. Yet the smallest of these particles—electrons—are the reason that the periodic table has a periodic pattern.

The electron shells around an atom's nucleus are different energy levels. Each energy level or shell can only hold so many electrons, depending on how far away it is from the nucleus. For example, the first shell can hold two electrons, while the second shell can hold eight electrons.

As mentioned earlier, the number of protons must balance the number of electrons in an atom. Take a look at hydrogen and helium in the first row of the periodic table. Hydrogen has one proton (its atomic number is one), so it needs one electron to balance this proton. Helium has two protons (its atomic number is two), so it needs two electrons to balance this proton. In both cases, the necessary electrons will fit into the first electron shell, since it can hold up to two electrons.

The second row begins with lithium with three protons, or atomic number 3. Lithium needs three electrons to balance its three protons. The first two can fit into shell 1, but the third electron must go into shell 2.

As the second row of the periodic table moves from lithium to neon, the number of protons and electrons in each element

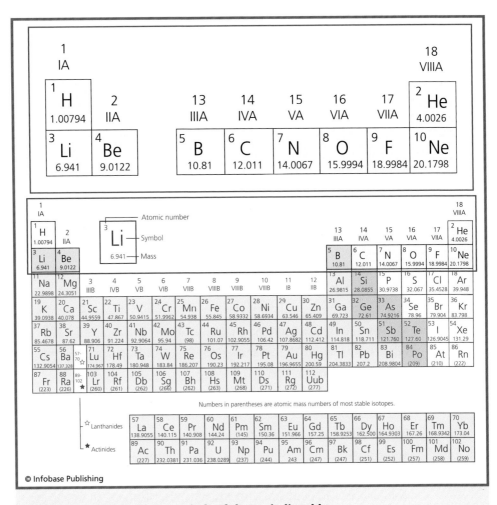

Figure 3.1   The first two periods of the periodic table.

increases. As the number of electrons increases, shell 2 quickly fills up. At neon (atomic number 10), shells 1 (two electrons) and 2 (eight electrons) are both full.

But now what? Sodium, which starts the third row, has 11 electrons. The first 10 can go into shells 1 and 2, but the leftover electron has to go into shell 3.

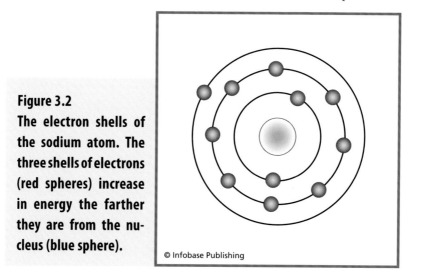

**Figure 3.2
The electron shells of
the sodium atom. The
three shells of electrons
(red spheres) increase
in energy the farther
they are from the nu-
cleus (blue sphere).**

© Infobase Publishing

This glimpse at the first elements in the table indicates a certain
pattern. Electrons fill up energy shells around each atom's nucleus
according to this pattern.

PERIODIC PATTERNS AND CHEMICAL REACTIONS

Electrons, especially the electrons that move about in an atom's
outermost shell, are the "face" that atoms show to the world.
The electrons in this **valence shell** are the ones most likely to be
involved in interactions with other atoms. In fact, chemical reactions are the result of atoms giving up electrons from their valence
shell, luring electrons away from other atoms to join their valence
shell, or sharing electrons in this shell with another atom.

Atoms with their outermost shells filled, such as neon and all
the other elements in the far right column of the periodic table, are
very stable and can last for long periods of time without changing.
Elements like lithium that have a mostly empty outermost shell 2
(only one electron) are likely to give that electron away to another
element in a chemical reaction. This reaction leaves lithium more
stable, with a completely filled shell 1 as its outermost shell.

Is there an easy way to tell whether an element will be reactive or nonreactive? Again, the pattern of the periodic table can help with the answer. Each element in the first column of the table (except for hydrogen, a special case that will be discussed later) represents the start of a new electron shell. Lithium's third electron

WHERE ARE THE LAKES IN THE PERIODIC TABLE?

Most elements in the periodic table are solids at room temperature. The atoms in these elements are tightly packed together, and the element holds its own shape. Eleven elements are gases at room temperature, including all of Group 18 and hydrogen, oxygen, nitrogen, chlorine, and fluorine. Gases are loose collections of atoms that spread out to fill a container of any size or shape. Bromine and mercury are the only two elements that are liquids at room temperature. Liquids are a state of matter between gases and solids. The atoms in a liquid are not as tightly packed as in a solid, but they stick closely together compared to atoms in a gas. Liquids can fill a container of any shape, but they do not expand to fill a container the way a gas does.

If we imagine the periodic table as an actual land, complete with valleys, mountains and deserts, bromine and mercury would be the "lakes," according to chemist P.W. Atkins. In his book *The Periodic Kingdom*, Atkins writes about the periodic table as if it were an imaginary land. Other scientists have pictured the periodic table in this way. For instance, the Royal Society of Chemistry in England has built a Web site of "pictures" of the periodic landscape (http://www.chemsoc.org/viselements/), showing mountains and cliffs where elements with a high atomic number stand.

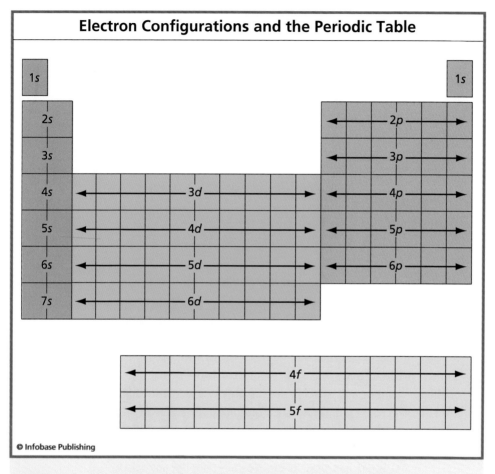

Figure 3.3   The periodic table showing the various blocks of orbitals.

is the first electron and only electron in shell 2. Sodium's eleventh electron is the first electron and only electron in shell 3, and so on down the column. Each of these elements is very reactive because they try to give away these lonely outermost electrons, known as **valence electrons**, to other elements.

Across a row, as the number of protons (and electrons) increases and the valence shell fills up, elements become less reactive. In general, this means that elements in columns at the left side of the table are very reactive and become less reactive as the columns move from left to right. Elements in columns act similarly in chemical reactions, simply because they are showing the same kind of electron face to other elements.

There is one more complication to the electron shells. Inside the shells themselves, electrons can be found in regions called **orbitals**. There are four types of orbitals—s, p, d, and f—and each has a specific shape. Blocks of the periodic table correspond to the different orbitals. The electrons in atoms of the first row of the table are found in the $1s$ orbital. Helium, at the far right of the first row, consists of 2 electrons in the $1s$ orbital. Neon, at the far right of the second row, has two electrons in the $1s$ orbital, 2 electrons in the $2s$ orbital, and 6 electrons in the $2p$ orbital. These arrangements of electrons within orbitals are known as electron configurations. Chemists notate the electron configuration of helium as $1s^2$ and neon as $1s^2 2s^2 2p^6$.

NAVIGATING THE TABLE

Reading the periodic table takes a little practice. To begin with, each element has its own box with two key numbers. The atomic number of the element, or the number of protons its atoms contain, is at the top of the box. (See the table in the Appendix on pages 92–93). Below the atomic number is the element's symbol letter or letters. The element's name is printed below the symbol, and underneath the name is the atomic weight. Element boxes on some periodic tables may include only the element symbol and atomic number.

Each row of the table is called a **period**. All of the elements in a period have the same number of electron shells. Columns in the table are called **groups**. For most groups, all of the elements have the same number of electrons in their outermost electron shell. In some places, such as the long "bridge" in the middle of the table,

TURNING THE TABLE

The periodic table, as it looks today, is a familiar part of classrooms and laboratories. But over the years, some scientists have rearranged the table into

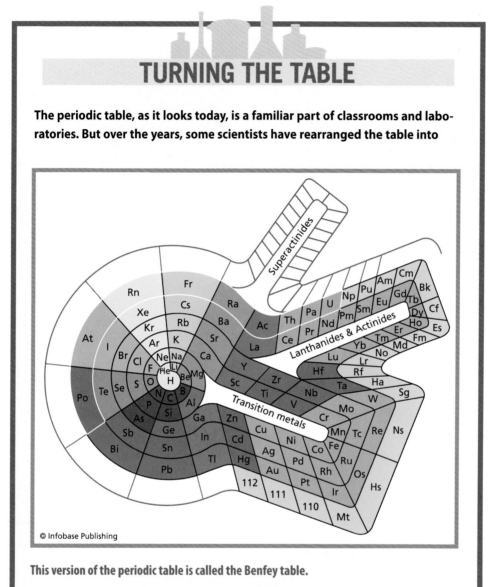

This version of the periodic table is called the Benfey table.

different shapes. Researchers have built pyramids, spirals, step tables, towers, and even galaxies to show how the elements are related to each other. In one triangular version, pathways between elements show how electron shells are filled. A key-shaped version shows the elements as one continuous spiral. Scientists also build periodic tables that highlight what they think is important about the elements in their particular field. For instance, one periodic table built especially for geologists and others who study earth sciences is based on the ions that elements form in nature.

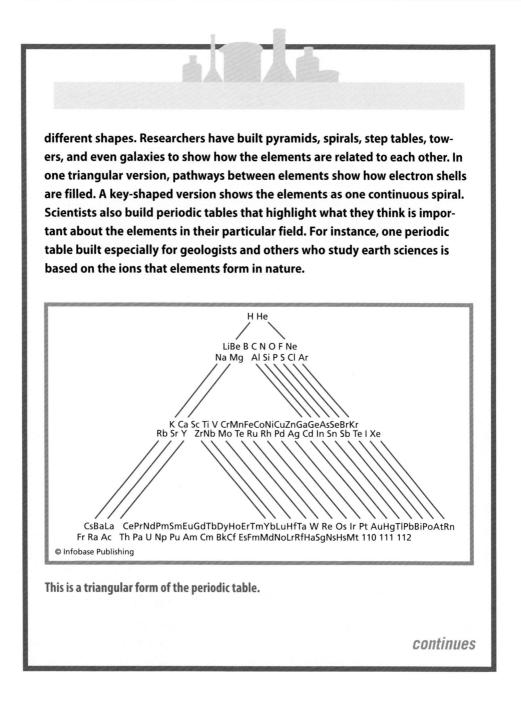

© Infobase Publishing

This is a triangular form of the periodic table.

continues

continued from page 27

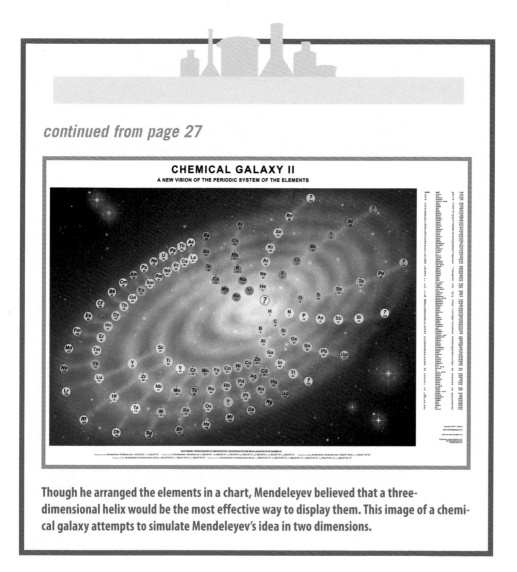

CHEMICAL GALAXY II
A NEW VISION OF THE PERIODIC SYSTEM OF THE ELEMENTS

Though he arranged the elements in a chart, Mendeleyev believed that a three-dimensional helix would be the most effective way to display them. This image of a chemical galaxy attempts to simulate Mendeleyev's idea in two dimensions.

several columns are included in the same group even though they have different numbers of electrons in their outermost shell.

At the bottom of the periodic table, there are two periods of elements with the atomic numbers 57–70 and 89–102. As the table shows, these elements really should be included in periods 6 and 7. Keeping them in these periods would make the table too long to print, so most of the time they are listed at the end to save space. These elements do have some unique features, as well.

Another way to look at the periodic table is to divide the elements into **metals, nonmetals,** and **metalloids**. Most of the elements in the table are metals. Metals are usually shiny and can be bent, hammered, or pulled into many different shapes without breaking into pieces. Metals are also good **conductors**, which means that heat and electricity can pass through them easily. Metals tend to give up electrons when they react with other elements. From this information, one could guess that most metals are found on the left side of the table, where the valence electron shells are mostly empty.

Nonmetals are not good conductors of electricity. They tend to gain or share electrons when they react with other elements, which places them closer to the right side of the table, where valence electron shells are full or almost full.

Metalloids are sometimes called **semiconductors**. These elements can conduct electricity, although not as well as metals. They may gain or lose electrons when they react with other elements. The most famous semiconductor element is silicon, which is used to make computer chips. Metalloids are found between metals and nonmetals on the periodic table.

SUMMARY

An atom is the smallest particle of an element that still has all the properties of that element. Atoms are made up of three main particles. Protons and neutrons come together in an atom's nucleus, whereas electrons orbit the nucleus. The number of protons in an atom determines what type of element it is. The structure of the periodic table comes from the fact that electron shells are filled in a specific pattern. The rows of the table are called *periods* and the columns are called *groups*. There are other ways to divide up the table, as well.

Alkali Metals and Alkaline Earth Metals

Elements in the first two groups of the periodic table are some of the most reactive elements known. In fact, many of the elements are so reactive that water, or in some cases air, can cause them to explode or catch fire. Although many of their names are familiar—sodium, potassium, and calcium, for instance—it is rare to find these elements on their own. Instead, these elements are usually combined with another more stable element to create a **compound**. Sodium chloride, or table salt, is a good example of a compound.

Group 1 elements, beginning with lithium (Li) and running vertically to francium (Fr), are called **alkali metals**. Group 2 elements, beginning with beryllium (Be) and running vertically to radium (Ra), are called the **alkaline earth metals**.

Hydrogen (H) is usually included at the top of the alkali metals, though it is not a metal. Like the Group 1 elements, however, hydrogen also has only one electron in its outermost shell. This

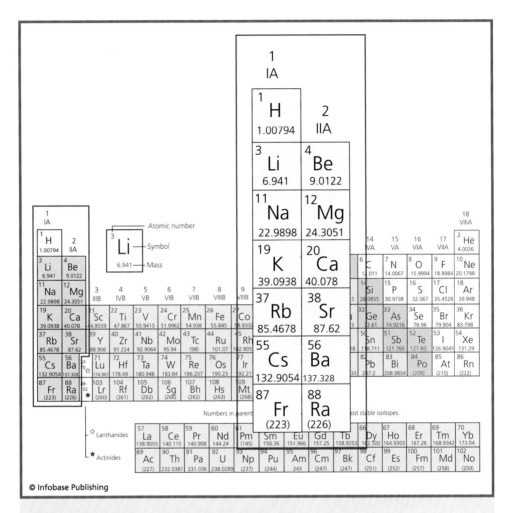

Figure 4.1   Groups 1 and 2 of the periodic table.

single electron in the outermost shell makes these elements very reactive. Eager to give up their lonely electron in favor of a full outermost shell, these elements easily combine with others. Alkaline earth metals are slightly less reactive, since they have two electrons in their valence shell.

In both groups, the metals are usually silver-colored but give off brilliant colors when burned. Compounds made with alkaline

Figure 4.2   Water falls onto pure sodium metal and creates a fiery chemical reaction. Pure alkali metals such as sodium are quite volatile. Because of this, alkali metals are generally stored in oil or wax.

earth metals are often used in fireworks. These metals are also very soft. In their pure form, unmixed with any other element, some of the alkali metals can be cut as if they were a stick of butter. But cutting or handling these pure metals is a tricky task. Pure sodium metal starts to break down when it is exposed to air. Exposed to water, sodium produces hydrogen gas that sometimes catches fire. Pure potassium and cesium metals explode violently in water and potassium may catch fire in open air. Pure alkali metals are usually stored in oil or wax to keep them from exploding.

Together, the alkali metals and alkaline earth metals are sometimes called the *s* **block**. The name comes from the fact that the valence electrons in these elements come from the *s* orbital.

WORKS WELL WITH OTHERS

Several alkali and alkaline earth metals are important to the human body and industrial applications, but most of the time they need a more stable element partner to be useful. For instance, calcium pairs with phosphorus to build bones and mixes with aluminum and silicon to make cement. Lime, a compound of calcium and oxygen, was used as a building material as far back as Roman times. Compounds made with sodium and potassium send electrical messages throughout the body, but can also be used to make glass, streetlights, and fertilizer for plants. Sodium is probably the best-known and widely used alkali metal. It combines with several other elements to make baking soda, the detergent ingredient borax, the food preservative sodium sulfite, and sodium hydroxide to clear clogged drains, among other compounds.

Magnesium combines with nitrogen and other elements to make chlorophyll, the green pigment that plants use to soak up sunlight. On the other hand, a combination of magnesium and the element fluorine is used to **polarize** sunglasses, windows, and other types of glass to reduce the glare of sunlight. Polarized materials change the way light waves pass through a material such as glass. In other compounds, magnesium helps produce bright flares and explosive devices. Magnesium was a key ingredient in some of the bombs that unleashed firestorms in European cities during World War II. Magnesium's terrible fires are very hard to stop and can only be extinguished with large amounts of dirt or sand rather than water.

Many compounds involving the alkali and alkaline earth metals are used as **desiccants**, or chemicals that can remove water from a material. Lithium hydride, potassium carbonate, calcium

PAY ME IN SALT

Sodium chloride—table salt—makes everything from french fries to popcorn taste better. But is a sprinkle of salt as valuable as money? People all over the ancient world thought it was. In the eleventh century A.D., people in China stamped little cakes of salt with a royal seal and used them like coins. Roman soldiers were given personal supplies of salt as part of their pay. The word "salary" comes from the Latin words *salarium argentum*, or "salt money."

Unpopular taxes on salt have also played an important role in more recent history. French farmers, angry at a large tax on salt that they were forced to buy from the government, helped overthrow the king and queen in the French Revolution. In the years leading up to the American Revolution, American colonists were unhappy with the British government for putting a high sales tax on salt. In 1930, the Indian leader Mahatma Gandhi and thousands of his countrymen made a famous march to the Arabian Sea to protest salt taxes by the British colonial government that ruled India at the time.

chloride, and barium acetate are all used as desiccants. For instance, calcium chloride is sometimes spread along roads to keep the dust down by holding a thin layer of water on the road surface that traps dust particles.

The Group 1 and 2 metals are lightweight and combine well with other lightweight but more stable metals such as aluminum. A mixture, or **alloy**, of aluminum and lithium is used in airplanes and racing bike frames. Lithium is often used to make light batteries for laptop computers, digital cameras, and pacemakers. Beryllium

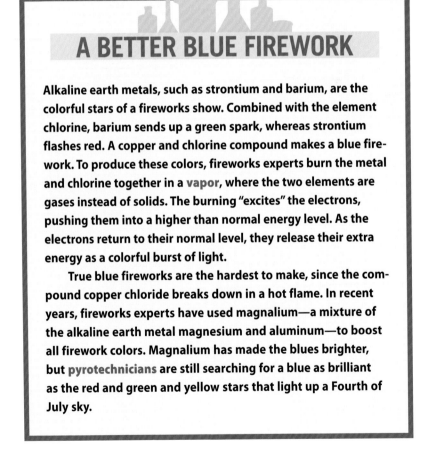

A BETTER BLUE FIREWORK

Alkaline earth metals, such as strontium and barium, are the colorful stars of a fireworks show. Combined with the element chlorine, barium sends up a green spark, whereas strontium flashes red. A copper and chlorine compound makes a blue firework. To produce these colors, fireworks experts burn the metal and chlorine together in a vapor, where the two elements are gases instead of solids. The burning "excites" the electrons, pushing them into a higher than normal energy level. As the electrons return to their normal level, they release their extra energy as a colorful burst of light.

True blue fireworks are the hardest to make, since the compound copper chloride breaks down in a hot flame. In recent years, fireworks experts have used magnalium—a mixture of the alkaline earth metal magnesium and aluminum—to boost all firework colors. Magnalium has made the blues brighter, but pyrotechnicians are still searching for a blue as brilliant as the red and green and yellow stars that light up a Fourth of July sky.

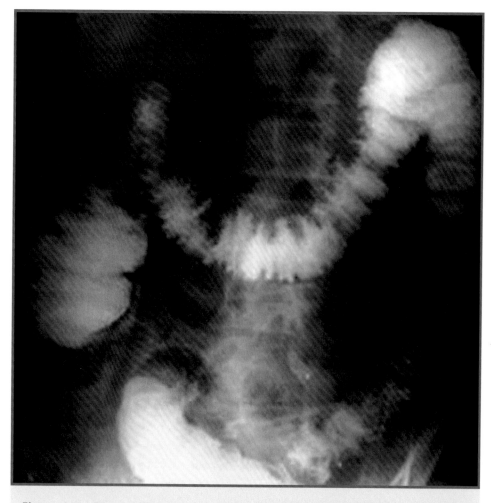

Figure 4.3   Doctors illuminate the intestines of a patient with the help of the alkaline earth metal barium. The patient drinks a concoction of barium sulfate that lines the stomach and intestines. Barium's chemical properties allow it to absorb X-rays, highlighting any problem areas.

is another lightweight metal used in satellites, aircraft, and nuclear weapons. (Beryllium is also the element that gives the gemstones beryl, emerald, and aquamarine their well-known blue-green color.) Magnesium also makes a good alloy metal for lightweight machines, such as lawn mowers and tools.

There are a few surprising medical uses among the alkali and alkaline earth metals. Lithium combined with chlorine has been used for decades to treat a form of depression called *bipolar disorder*. Scientists are not exactly sure how lithium affects depression, but they think it may somehow change chemical messages in the brain. Doctors use barium, one of the heaviest alkaline earth metals, to get a better look at the stomach and intestines. They give their patients a drink called *barium sulfate* that travels to the gut. Barium's 56 electrons absorb X-rays and light up the stomach and intestines to reveal ulcers and other problems.

There are a few elements in these two groups that sometimes cause health problems because they are very similar to nearby elements. For instance, a toxic type of strontium can increase the risk of bone cancer and leukemia. Strontium, just one space below calcium in the table, is so similar to calcium that the body is sometimes fooled into absorbing it like calcium in bones and teeth. The similarities between elements can also be useful, as in the case of potassium chloride. People with high blood pressure and certain heart or kidney diseases need less sodium in their diets to stay healthy. Instead of sprinkling regular table salt or sodium chloride on their meals, they may use potassium chloride for a very similar salty taste.

WHERE DOES HYDROGEN BELONG?

Hydrogen has earned its atomic number 1. It is the most abundant element in space, making up 90% of all atoms in the universe. Scientists think hydrogen was the first element to form when the universe was born in the Big Bang. The most common form of hydrogen only has one proton and one electron. Its simple structure is the base on which all other elements are built.

Hydrogen's special position among the elements makes it an orphan in the periodic table. Most periodic tables place hydrogen above lithium in the alkali metals. The reason, as discussed above, is that hydrogen has one electron in its outermost shell like the rest of the alkali metals. (Actually, hydrogen has only one shell.)

Some scientists, however, think that hydrogen really belongs on top of fluorine in Group 17. Instead of hydrogen having a mostly empty electron shell, they argue, it has a nearly full shell—one electron away from being complete, just like the elements in Group 17. Other tables float hydrogen above the rest of the elements, since

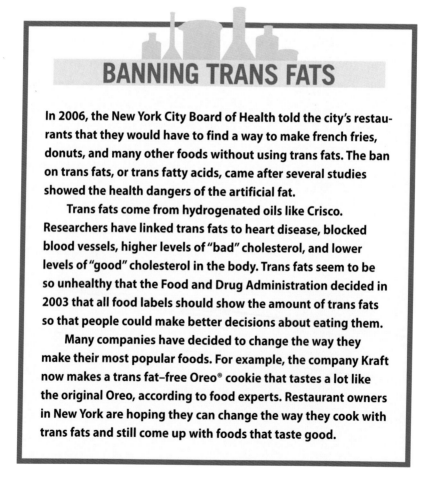

BANNING TRANS FATS

In 2006, the New York City Board of Health told the city's restaurants that they would have to find a way to make french fries, donuts, and many other foods without using trans fats. The ban on trans fats, or trans fatty acids, came after several studies showed the health dangers of the artificial fat.

Trans fats come from hydrogenated oils like Crisco. Researchers have linked trans fats to heart disease, blocked blood vessels, higher levels of "bad" cholesterol, and lower levels of "good" cholesterol in the body. Trans fats seem to be so unhealthy that the Food and Drug Administration decided in 2003 that all food labels should show the amount of trans fats so that people could make better decisions about eating them.

Many companies have decided to change the way they make their most popular foods. For example, the company Kraft now makes a trans fat–free Oreo® cookie that tastes a lot like the original Oreo, according to food experts. Restaurant owners in New York are hoping they can change the way they cook with trans fats and still come up with foods that taste good.

it does not react in exactly the same way as any other group in the table.

Floating or anchored, hydrogen is one of the most important elements for life on Earth. It forms more compounds than any other element. The strong bonds it forms with oxygen keep water molecules from boiling away on the Earth's surface. Hydrogen bonds also make up the backbone of **DNA**, the molecule that holds the genetic information of every living thing.

Hydrogen has its industrial uses as well. Nearly two-thirds of the world's manufactured hydrogen is used to make ammonia (a combination of the elements nitrogen and hydrogen) for fertilizer. Hydrogen is also used in rocket fuel and in the chemical reactions that fuel nuclear reactions and hydrogen bombs. Hydrogen plays a more notorious role in the creation of hydrogenated vegetable oil. Hydrogen turns these oils into solid fats at room temperature that are most often used in fried and baked foods to make them taste better and last longer on grocery shelves. Medical researchers, however, have singled out hydrogenated oils in recent years as one possible cause of heart disease.

Hydrogen may also be a clean fuel of the future, one that produces almost no pollution when it burns in a car or other engine. Although hydrogen could replace gasoline as the fuel that is burned in a car engine, most manufacturers are instead testing cars that run on hydrogen **fuel cells**. A fuel cell turns hydrogen into electricity that could power a car. Fuel cell technology for cars, buses, and other vehicles seems promising, but so far the fuel cells are expensive to make and are very fragile.

RADIOACTIVITY: THE NUCLEUS FALLS APART

In the 1920s, women working in a New Jersey factory painted watch faces with an element called *radium* that glowed in the dark. The women constantly straightened their paintbrush bristles between their lips to keep them pointed enough to draw the tiny numbers. A few years later, the women began to have strange sores, pains all

Figure 4.4 "The Radium Girls" were women in 1920s New Jersey who painted watch faces with radium, an element that glows in the dark. Because the women were in constant contact with the radioactive element, they experienced numerous health problems years later. Some even died because of radiation poisoning.

over the body, and crumbling bones. Several of the women died soon afterward.

"The Radium Girls," as they came to be known, were suffering from radiation poisoning. The glowing powder that they painted on their nails and teeth for fun was a chemical time bomb waiting to rip through their cells. Years after radium's discovery in 1898 by French chemists Marie and Pierre Curie, the girls had accidentally stumbled on the terrible power of **radioactivity**.

Radioactivity consists of tiny energy particles that are produced when the nucleus of an atom becomes unstable and falls apart.

Typically, the nucleus of an atom is glued together by a force that attracts protons to each other. When the nucleus has too many protons or not enough neutrons, this force is overwhelmed and the nucleus falls apart, or decays.

Many elements have radioactive isotopes, or versions of themselves where the number of protons and neutrons in their nuclei has somehow become imbalanced. Unstable nuclei are more likely in larger atoms with their larger amounts of protons, because the forces pushing those protons away from each other are much stronger than the force attracting them together.

Once again, the periodic table offers clues about which elements could be radioactive naturally. All of the elements in Period 7—like francium in the alkali metals and radium in the alkaline earth metals—are large atoms with many protons. All of the Period 7 elements are radioactive.

Radiation—the energy particles released by radioactive elements—can be a friend or foe to the human body. As The Radium Girls discovered, radiation can destroy cells and change the DNA in cells in a way that increases the risk of cancer. Yet radiation therapy is also widely used as a treatment for cancer, because carefully targeted radiation can be used to kill cancer cells.

Years of working with radioactive elements in the lab left Marie and Pierre Curie very sick as well. In 1934, Marie Curie died of a blood disease caused by exposure to radiation. When scientists examined her lab notebooks many decades later, they uncovered her glowing and toxic fingerprints everywhere.

The steady decay of radioactive elements has some other important uses. One radioactive form of cesium releases radiation at such a steady rate that the world's most accurate clocks rely on this rate to keep time. Another timekeeper is the precise decay of radioactive potassium into the more stable element argon. Scientists use potassium-argon dating to determine the age of rocks and stone tools at ancient human sites that are more than a million years old. The researchers know how long it takes all the potassium in a rock to turn to argon, so they measure the amount of potassium left in the rock to come up with its age.

SUMMARY

The alkali metals are found in Group 1 of the periodic table. The alkaline earth metals are found in Group 2 of the table. Elements in these two groups are soft, highly reactive metals. They are most useful to humans in compounds with other elements. The gas hydrogen is often grouped with the alkali metals, though it has special properties of its own. The larger an atom gets, the more likely it is that its nucleus will become unstable and begin to break down. The energy released in this process is called *radioactivity*.

Transition Metals

When people are asked to name any element, the chances are good that they will come up with the name of a **transition metal**. Transition metals are found in numerous products, such as coins, jewelry, light bulbs, cars, and even some surprising places such as sunscreen and cell phones. Most people see, touch, and depend on transition metals hundreds of times each day.

The transition metals are the "bridge" of the periodic table, including Groups 3 through 12 and Periods 4 through 7. There is a strange break within the transition metals at elements 57 and 89 in Group 3. The break marks the beginning of the **lanthanides** and the **actinides.** On the basis of their atomic numbers, these two unusual sets of elements seem to fit into the transition metal bridge. They do not act like transition metals, however, so most periodic tables pull these elements out of atomic number

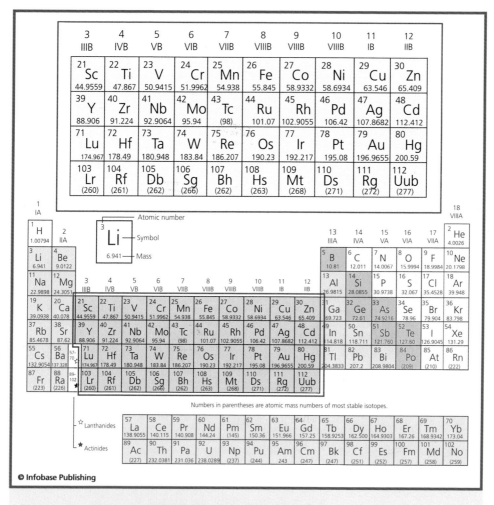

© Infobase Publishing

Figure 5.1   The transition metals of the periodic table.

order and give them their own home at the bottom of the table.

There is a reason—several reasons, actually—why the transition metals include so many elements with recognizable names, like gold, iron, zinc, and titanium. The first clue is in their name: transition metals. All of the transition metal elements are metals.

They have the traits of metals, such as the ability to conduct electricity and the ability to be worked into different shapes.

What does transition mean? A transition is a change from one thing to another. Yttrium (atomic number 39) is a very different metal from silver (atomic number 47). Even though the transition elements are all metals, Group 3 metals act very differently from Group 12 metals.

The transition metals change gradually as one moves from left to right across the bridge. On the left side of the bridge, the elements have only a few electrons moving through their valence shell. Atoms with these mostly empty valence shells are more reactive, or more likely to give up the few electrons they have if they happen to encounter other atoms. This means that a transition metal like silver, which tends to hold on to its valence electrons, is less reactive than a transition metal like yttrium. The wide range of possible chemical reactions gives chemists and engineers many possibilities when it comes to making things out of transition metals.

Another way to look at the transition metal bridge is to think of it as a path between metals and nonmetals. As the electron shells fill up from left to right across the periods, the elements become less like metals and more like the nonmetals to their right, especially the nonmetals in Groups 14 through 17.

There is one other unusual thing about the transition metals, and it involves their valence shell electrons. Unlike most elements, the valence electrons of transition metals are not in their outermost electron shell, but from their next-to-outermost shell. The valence electrons move through the *d* orbital in this shell, making the transition metals the ***d* block** of the periodic table.

All of these features give the transition metals some very useful properties. The metals tend to be hard, shiny, and strong. It takes high temperatures to melt and boil most of them. Most transition metals do a good job of conducting electricity and heat. Many of the elements can bind to oxygen in more than one way, which can create many different compounds. Because the transition metals can interact with other elements—and especially oxygen—in a variety of ways, they make good **catalysts**, or helpers that can trigger or speed up a chemical reaction. Although these metals are strong and hard, they are not brittle. They can be stretched into thin wires or pounded flat or bent in a variety of ways without breaking. For instance, a piece of gold about the size of a grain of rice can be flattened into a sheet of gold about 10 square feet (.93 square meters), big enough to carpet a small bedroom—although that carpet would be only a few atoms thick.

INDUSTRIAL GIANTS

There are transition metals in many of the products that people use in daily life. Some of these metals have obvious roles, such as the coin metals of gold, silver, and copper. Iron, which makes up 90% of all metal that is **refined**, or purified for use, is found in everything from tools to paper staples to washing machines. The most important iron product is **steel**, an iron-based metal alloy. Most steel made for manufacturing purposes is iron alloyed with the element carbon, which makes the steel much harder than iron alone. Several other transition metals are alloyed with iron to make different kinds of steel for different uses. Vanadium, niobium, molybdenum, manganese, chromium, and nickel are all used in steel alloys. For instance, chromium and nickel are alloyed with iron to create stainless steel, a type of steel that does not rust and is used in surgical instruments, cookware, and tools. Some famous landmarks such as the top of the Chrysler skyscraper in New York City and the St. Louis Gateway Arch are covered in stainless steel.

Another industrially important transition metal is titanium, which is used especially to make light but strong industrial parts, such as pipes and airplane propellers. When it is exposed to the air, titanium reacts with oxygen to form a thin layer of titanium dioxide, a compound of titanium and oxygen. The titanium dioxide protects the metal against **corrosion**, or the gradual breakdown of the metal by environmental conditions such as salt water and strong gases. This unique feature makes titanium very useful in submarines and offshore oil rigs. The swooping walls of the

WAR, GORILLAS, AND CELL PHONES

In the Democratic Republic of the Congo, people go to war, children drop out of school to work long hours in muddy riverbanks, and rare gorillas are butchered for food. A world away, schoolchildren use their cell phones to text friends or head home after school to play video games. Is there a connection between these two things? There is—an element called *tantalum*. The high-tech world of computers and cell phones depends on tantalum to protect metal coatings on computer chips and to make tiny electricity storage devices called *capacitors*. Although it is rarely found on its own, tantalum can be extracted from an ore called columbite-tantalite or coltan.

That is where the problem arises. One of the world's biggest sources of coltan is in the Democratic Republic of the Congo, an impoverished African nation where most people live on about 20 cents a day. As more people around the world use cell phones and computers, manufacturers need more coltan and are willing to pay high prices to get it.

People in the Congo and neighboring African countries are now fighting over coltan deposits, often killing their rivals and destroying large parts of the tropical rainforest to get at the valuable ore. International groups like the United Nations say the fighting is a disaster for the country. They have asked cell phone and computer companies to be more careful about buying tantalum from places like the Congo, where the element has resulted in much violence.

Guggenheim art museum in Bilbao, Spain, one of the most famous modern buildings in the world, are covered in corrosion-resistant titanium panels.

Copper is another transition metal that does not corrode easily, which makes it useful for water pipes. Copper is also an excellent conductor of heat, which explains why copper-bottomed cooking pans have been used for centuries. Today, most copper is used in electrical wiring, since it conducts electricity so well and can be stretched into thin shapes. Other transition metals that resist corrosion include platinum, osmium, and iridium. These last two elements are often used in metal pen nibs (the tip of a fountain ink pen) and the tip of spark plugs for cars.

These common uses only hint at all the things that transition metals can do. The "copper" penny, for instance, is mostly made of zinc, another transition metal. Chromium provides the shiny, mirror-like metal coating on "chrome" car bumpers, but is also added to some lasers to make their light shine red. Nickel and chromium combine in an alloy that can be coiled into the wires that heat toasters and hair dryers. Titanium dioxide is a very white reflective compound used in toothpaste and paints. The transition metal cadmium is used in brilliant and permanent colors such as cadmium yellow, red, and orange. Artists have used cadmium-based paints for hundreds of years, and manufacturers used the colors more recently in plastic products. However, the colors are rarely used now that scientists have discovered that cadmium pollution can cause cancer and other health problems.

The transition metal cobalt has its own artistic history; it is used to give a deep blue or sometimes green color to pottery and glass. Anyone who has played with a toy chemistry set has probably made "invisible ink," another unusual cobalt product. Invisible ink is made from a compound of cobalt and chlorine. Dissolved in a mixture of water and a common liquid called *glycerine*, the ink becomes colorless. When a message written in the ink is heated, the water and glycerine break away from the cobalt compound and allow its original dark color to mysteriously reappear.

Everyday products also depend on less-familiar transition metals. The filament in light bulbs—the tiny thread that heats up and gives off light inside the bulb—is made of the element tungsten. Tungsten can be stretched into a very thin wire, making it perfect for light bulbs. Inside each 60 watt light bulb is a 6-foot (1.93 meter)

BACTERIAL GOLDDIGGERS

In 2006, scientists working at the Tomakin Park Gold Mine and the Hit or Miss Gold Mine in Queensland, Australia took a closer look at gold grains found in the soil around the mines. These scattered grains and nuggets are usually called *secondary gold deposits,* because they are not part of the big deposits of gold that form inside rocks.

Erosion can break big gold deposits into secondary gold grains, but researcher Frank Reith and his fellow scientists noticed something strange about the secondary grains at the Australian mines. Most of the gold grains were coated with bacterial slime, and some of the grains actually looked like bacteria. Oddly, the soil around the grains did not have any of the same bacterial slime in it.

What's the connection between gold and slime? The scientists think a bacterium called *Ralstonia metallidurans* is actually building these small gold nuggets from scratch. Tiny amounts of gold can be toxic for *Ralstonia,* so the bacteria have come up with a way to avoid it. They pull the metal from the surrounding soil into their cells and release it in the form of gold grains. In some cases, the gold coats the outside of the bacterium, leaving a gold-plated, bacteria-shaped nugget behind in the soil.

tungsten wire, coiled up to fit within an inch (2.5 centimeters) of space. Yttrium oxide, a compound of the transition metal yttrium and oxygen, is used to make the red color inside the picture tubes of a color television. Silver, mostly known as a jewelry metal, also has the unusual job of rainmaker. Particles of silver iodide, a compound of silver and iodine that has a shape very similar to ice crystals, are sometimes sprayed or "seeded" into clouds to encourage the formation of rain droplets.

Another unusual pairing of transition metals happens in floodlights like those used in football and baseball stadiums. In arena lights, mercury vapor is combined with the compound scandium iodide (a combination of the transition metal scandium and the element iodine) to make the bright lights seem more like natural sunlight. Television shows and movies also use these kinds of lights for night filming.

Iridium is a lesser-known transition metal, but it has become a famous clue in the mystery of how and why the dinosaurs became extinct 65 million years ago. There is an unusually large amount of iridium in rock layers all over the world that date to the time of the dinosaur die-off. In 1980, a team of scientists suggested that the iridium came from a huge meteorite that struck the Earth 65 million years ago, creating firestorms and throwing up a huge dust cloud all around the planet. Many other plants and animals disappeared at the same time as the dinosaurs, and so far the massive meteorite strike is one of the most convincing explanations for all these extinctions.

Transition metals have proved so useful throughout history that it is not surprising to find them right in the middle of some exciting plans for the future. For instance, engineers have already built a train that floats over its tracks while speeding along at more than 300 miles an hour. It sounds like science fiction, but the trains are powered by a strong magnetic force produced by coils of superconducting metal. In a **superconductor**, electricity flows freely without anything holding it back and scattering its energy. The transition

Figure 5.2 **Scientists have created a means of revolutionary train travel. The "levitation" train travels over superconducting metal. This metal concentrates electricity so that it becomes an intense magnetic field. Magnetic parts in the train make the train levitate and travel at speeds close to 350 miles per hour.**

metal yttrium is one of the key elements in superconducting compounds like those used in "levitating" trains.

MEDICAL MARVELS

In the 1960s, scientists performing experiments on bacteria accidentally discovered a strange effect in their lab. They grew bacteria in electric fields to see how the fields affected the bacteria's dividing cells. The bacteria started growing into long strings made up of cells that were getting bigger but not dividing. After careful investigation, the researchers found that the transition metal platinum used in the experiment was reacting with other chemicals to make a compound called *cisplatin*. It was cisplatin that kept the cells from dividing normally.

The scientists quickly realized that cisplatin could be a useful drug against some kinds of cancer, where cells often divide in abnormal ways. Their studies led to a number of platinum-based anticancer drugs, including cisplatin, which are still used to fight tumors.

Many other transition metals have important uses in health and medicine. For instance, titanium is used to build more than airplanes. Surgeons also rely on the lightweight metal to screw together broken bones and build heart pacemakers. A radioactive version of the transition metal cobalt is used to kill harmful bacteria in some foods, like meat. Surfers and beach volleyball players slather their noses in zinc oxide compound (a combination of the transition metal zinc and the element oxygen) to stop sunburn. Gold and the transition metal palladium are widely used to build tooth crowns, the "cap" that dentists cement on top of a decayed tooth. Tooth fillings themselves are often an **amalgam**, a mixture of the transition metal mercury and other metals such as silver, tin, and copper. Although mercury can be harmful to human health, there is no evidence that these dental amalgams release enough mercury to be poisonous.

One of the strangest transition metals in modern medicine is technetium, which does not exist on Earth naturally. Its **half-life**, or the time that it takes for half of a sample of the element to break down, is so short that all the technetium created when the Earth formed has already disappeared. But scientists have found a way to bring it back from the dead. When an isotope of the element molybdenum—another transition metal—breaks down, it turns into an isotope of technetium that lasts for about 6 hours. The technetium isotope latches on to certain kinds of heart muscle and can be seen in the muscle with special machines, similar to an X-ray.

Doctors sometimes inject the technetium isotope to help them see exactly where a heart has been damaged after a heart attack.

Technetium and other transition metals can be lifesavers, but other metals in this part of the periodic table can threaten human health. Mercury, cadmium, and nickel are some of the transition metals that can cause problems ranging from skin allergies to toxic poisoning. Some people have also been concerned about the health risks of a mercury-containing compound in vaccines, the injections given to prevent diseases such as the flu. However, there is no evidence that this compound is unsafe, according to most medical experts.

SUMMARY

The transition metals are the elements found in Groups 3 through 12 and Periods 4 through 6 of the periodic table. Transition metals include a wide variety of metals that look and react differently depending on where they are placed within the groups. Most transition metals tend to be hard, shiny, and strong. The variety among these elements makes them important in countless products in the home, industry, and medicine.

Lanthanides, Actinides, and Transuranium Elements

The lower half of most modern periodic tables contains two rows that seem to float apart from the rest of the elements. These two rows are the lanthanides and actinides. By atomic number, they should fall into Periods 6 and 7 of the table. Some extra-long tables do squeeze them into these periods. But the lanthanide and actinide elements have a few special features that truly set them apart from the rest of the transition metals.

The lanthanide elements begin with lanthanum (atomic number 57) and go to ytterbium (atomic number 70). The actinide elements begin with actinium (atomic number 89) and go to nobelium (atomic number 102).

The actinides include another part of the periodic table called the *transuranium elements*, which begin with neptunium (atomic number 93) and end with roentgenium (atomic number 111) back up in Period 7. Neptunium and plutonium are the only

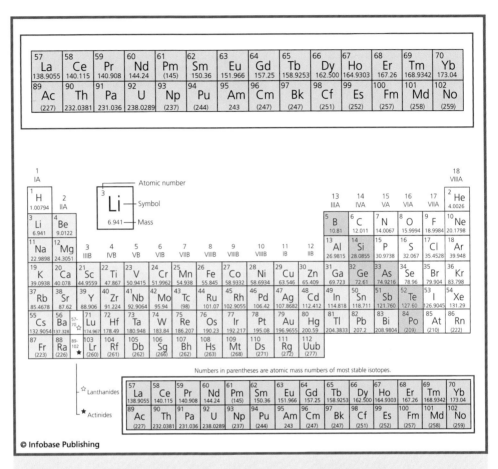

Figure 6.1   The lanthanides begin with lanthanum (atomic number 57) and end in ytterbium (atomic number 70). The actinides begin with actinium (atomic number 89) and end with nobelium (atomic number 102).

transuranium elements found in nature. The rest have all been created in a laboratory or discovered in the wreckage of atomic bombs. Transuranium elements are so highly radioactive that most of them are short-lived, breaking down within seconds or less.

The lanthanides and actinides, along with the rest of the transuranium elements, are all metals. Although they are listed apart from the transition metals, they still share some similarities with their fellow group members among those elements. For instance, lanthanum is similar to yttrium, which would be its upstairs neighbor in Group 3.

Like the transition metals, however, the lanthanides and actinides break the rules a little when it comes to their valence electron shell. Transition metals share electrons from the *d* orbital in their next-to-outermost shell. The valence electrons in lanthanides

SELF-MADE SCIENTIST: JAMES ANDREW HARRIS

Many chemists go to school for years and earn the top college degree before they make important discoveries in the lab, but James Andrew Harris took a different path. Harris graduated from college with a basic degree in chemistry, but then served in the Army and worked in a company lab before joining the team that discovered the transuranium elements rutherfordium and dubnium.

Harris was the first African American to work on the discovery of new elements. In a 1973 interview, he described how hard it could be for a black man to find work as a chemist. Employers would sometimes make him do simple adding and subtracting tests, because they did not believe he could do more complicated math and science problems.

Harris's talents were finally noticed at the University of California's Lawrence Radiation Laboratory, where he helped prepare some of the elements used in the discovery of rutherfordium and dubnium. Although he never finished his studies, his old college gave him a doctorate—the highest degree in science—to honor his work on the new elements.

and actinides are located even closer to the nucleus, in the third-to-outermost electron shell. They travel in the *f* orbital of this shell. For this reason, the lanthanide and actinide rows are also called the ***f* block** of the periodic table.

Adding electrons to a shell closer to the nucleus has a strange effect on the lanthanides. As the number of electrons and protons gets larger with each new lanthanide, the atoms themselves actually shrink, because the electrons are added close to the nucleus instead of filling up outer shells that would expand the atom's overall size. (Actinide atoms might shrink in the same way, but most actinides are too short-lived to have their size measured.)

NOT-SO-RARE EARTHS

The lanthanide elements were once known as the "rare earths." Lanthanides, however, are not particularly rare. Holmium, one of the less common lanthanides, is still 20 times more abundant than silver on Earth. The *rare earth* name comes instead from how difficult it was for early chemists to separate all of the lanthanides from one another. Because these elements add electrons to an inner shell, they all show the same "face" to other elements. This makes them all react very similarly with other elements, and it can be tricky to tell them apart.

Lanthanides such as lanthanum, europium, gadolinium, and terbium are used to give color and glow to searchlights, fluorescent light bulbs, color televisions, and computer monitors. Terbium compounds are behind the green color in television picture tubes and computer screens. Lanthanides like holmium, erbium, and neodymium are mixed into compounds to tint glass. Several lanthanide compounds show up in fiber optic cables and special lenses. Welders wear goggles that contain erbium and praseodymium in the lenses because the elements help absorb the strong light of the welding torch. One of the more unusual uses of a lanthanide is in printing postage stamps. A compound of the lanthanide europium and oxygen printed on stamps gives off a distinctive glow that can be "read" by mail sorting machines.

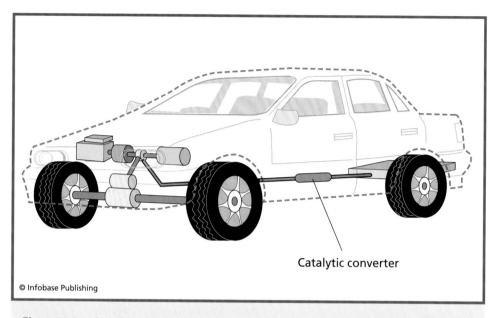

Catalytic converter

© Infobase Publishing

Figure 6.2   A car's catalytic converter treats the exhaust produced by its engine combustion, breaking down pollutants such as nitrogen oxides before they leave the car.

Several lanthanide metals can be found in certain types of magnetic data storage disks for computers. Gadolinium, terbium, and dysprosium are among the elements often sandwiched with iron and cobalt in thin layers to make these devices.

A compound of the lanthanide cerium and oxygen is used in catalytic converters, devices in cars that clean up the dirty fumes created by the engine. The walls of self-cleaning ovens also contain this compound. The cerium in the compound stores the oxygen until the oxygen is released to break down the polluting carbon and nitrogen gases pumped out of an engine or the carbon crust left by a baked casserole. A combination of several lanthanides and iron called *misch metal* is still used by some steel makers to clean up unwanted oxygen and sulfur that can weaken steel. Misch metal also throws a spark when it is scraped, making it useful in cigarette lighters.

The lanthanum neodymium plays an unusual part in outsmarting counterfeiters. Neodymium combined with iron and boron makes a powerful magnet called *a NIB magnet*. NIB magnets are so strong that they can latch on to the tiny metal particles that the United States weaves into its paper money. Most counterfeiters are not able to insert these metal particles into their fake money, so a NIB magnet will not stick to the counterfeit bills. NIB magnets are also part of automatic car door locks and windows and computer hard drives.

The lanthanides are no longer rare in the laboratory or in everyday life. Many chemists, however, still see them as a large collection of elements with few real differences between them.

ELEMENTS OF WAR

Usually the discovery of a new element is announced in a scientific paper or at a scientific meeting. The actinide elements curium and americium were announced to the world in a 1945 children's radio show called "Quiz Kids." The show's guest scientist on November 11 that year was a young scientist named Glenn Seaborg. One of the children on the show asked Seaborg if any new elements had been discovered lately. Seaborg happily shared the news that his lab had in fact created two new elements with atomic numbers 95 and 96.

In fact, Seaborg and his fellow scientists had discovered curium (named after Pierre and Marie Curie) and americium in 1944, but their findings were part of the United States' secret program to build an atomic bomb. When World War II ended in 1945 with two atomic bombs dropped on Japan, a handful of strange new elements were introduced to the world.

Natural actinides such as actinide, thorium, and especially uranium were already well known to chemists. Like other heavy elements, the actinides are very radioactive. Actinium itself is so radioactive that it glows in the dark. As Seaborg and others found

GLENN T. SEABORG   SHEILA CONLAN   BOB BURKE   NOV. 11, 1945

Figure 6.3   The elements curium and americium were introduced by way of a popular 1940s radio show called "Quiz Kids." The scientist Glenn Seaborg (left) appeared on the November 11, 1945, episode.

out, the particles released by unstable, radioactive actinides such as uranium can be turned into a deadly weapon.

In an atomic bomb, a single neutron can splinter a uranium atom and scatter its neutrons, which then fly away to split apart other atoms. This atomic splitting, or **fission**, releases a huge amount of energy—so much energy that an atomic bomb explosion can be as powerful as the blast of 500,000 tons of TNT.

The World War II scientists found out that new elements could also be created in these powerful explosions. Neptunium, plutonium, americium, and curium were discovered in the early atomic bomb experiments. Other actinides such as fermium and

Figure 6.4   This immense explosion is an example of a fusion bomb, one in which small atoms combine to create a larger atom. The effect of fusion can be much stronger than splitting atoms, or fission.

einsteinium were discovered in the exploded material of the first **fusion** bomb. In a fusion bomb, smaller atoms collide to create a bigger atom in a huge burst of energy that can be thousands of times stronger than a fission explosion.

Some of the elements of war have found a place in peacetime. The same kind of reaction in uranium that makes an atomic bomb explode can be controlled to make electricity in a nuclear power plant. The Cassini spacecraft now orbiting the planet Saturn runs on plutonium fuel. Plutonium-based fuel was also used to power devices that the Apollo 14 astronauts left on the Moon, such as a seismometer left to detect movements of the Moon's crust. The Voyager spacecraft also sent its golden record out to the stars with the help of plutonium fuel. In both cases, the heat created by plutonium's radioactive decay was turned into electrical power.

Americium is a critical ingredient in smoke detectors. Some of the tiny particles released by an americium compound create a small electric charge inside smoke detectors. Smoke or soot can block the charge, which sets off the alarm. One gram of americium is enough for 5,000 smoke detectors.

In the late nineteenth and early twentieth centuries, the actinide thorium played a part in lighting cities all across Europe and the United States. Woven cotton bags coated with thorium compounds burn with a bright light at high temperatures without melting, so they were used in gas-lit street lamps. Once scientists recognized the possible danger in using this radioactive metal (and electric lights became more popular), thorium street lamps disappeared. Today, some gas camping lanterns still contain thorium wicks, although most lantern manufacturers have switched over to yttrium or cerium compounds instead to produce the same glow.

SEARCHING FOR THE ISLAND OF STABILITY

The elements after fermium (atomic number 100) are sometimes called the **transfermian** or **superheavy elements**. All of them were created in the laboratory, some lasting only milliseconds before they break down. They do not have any special uses, but they do help scientists study what happens inside very heavy atoms.

To make a new element, scientists have to add protons to an element that already exists. (remember that an element is defined by how many protons it has in its nucleus.) Scientists sometimes do this by bombarding an element with neutrons. These free neutrons can break tiny particles off of the neutrons in an atom's nucleus and turn them into protons. In some cases, researchers use light particles such as the nuclei of helium atoms to bombard a target element. Some of the heaviest elements (above atomic number 106) were created in a kind of gentle "smashup" of a heavy element such as lead and a medium-weight element such as chromium. Protons from both elements collect in one superheavy atom as a result of the smashup.

HOPE, FRAUD, AND ELEMENT 118

A lot of things go into making a new superheavy element: the right target, the right technique, and a little a bit of luck. Scientists at Lawrence Berkeley National Laboratory thought all three things were working for them when they bombarded a lead target with krypton ions and saw signs of an element with 118 protons, the heaviest ever created.

The scientists announced their new discovery in 1999, sending chemists around the world running to their own laboratories to try the experiment for themselves. None of the scientists, however, could re-create the new element. When the Berkeley scientists themselves tried the experiment again, element 118 was nowhere to be found.

Confused, the Berkeley team carefully looked over the notes of their first experiment. The notes revealed an unhappy surprise. The evidence for element 118 did not appear in the original recordings of the experiment. One of the scientists on the team had faked the signs that seemed to point to the discovery of the new superheavy element.

The scientist was fired from his job at the lab. The other scientists on the team had to announce that they had not found element 118 after all. The case was so shocking that one magazine said the fraud was the science world's "breakdown of the year." But the strange case of element 118 did remind researchers of an important rule: Anyone should be able to repeat a good experiment.

The superheavy elements usually last for seconds or less because their nucleus is unstable, as is the nucleus of most heavy and radioactive elements. Nevertheless, chemists think there may be a way for the nucleus of a superheavy element to become more stable.

Inside the nucleus, protons and neutrons move in orbits or energy shells that are similar to the electron shells outside the nucleus. If these shells are filled with certain numbers of protons and neutrons, the nucleus becomes more stable than if the protons and neutrons just move around freely in the nucleus. Scientists who have studied these "magic numbers" say that elements 112 to 118 might have the right number of protons and neutrons to survive for longer periods of time without breaking down. This group of yet-to-be discovered elements is sometimes called the **island of stability**.

Could there be an end to the periodic table? Researchers think there probably is a limit to how big an atom can get before its electron orbits become unstable. Most scientists think the largest possible atomic number is between 170 and 210, although the nucleus itself may break down at atomic numbers much smaller than 170.

SUMMARY

The lanthanide and actinide elements are located at the bottom of the periodic table in two rows separate from the rest of the elements. By atomic number, they should be located in Periods 6 and 7, but they have special properties that distinguish them from elements in those periods. Lanthanides are very similar to each other and have some industrial uses. Many of the actinides were discovered as part of the first atomic bomb experiments. They are highly radioactive and have few uses. The transuranium elements were mostly created in the laboratory and are very short-lived.

Poor Metals, Metalloids, and Nonmetals: The BCNOs

The elements in Groups 13 through 16 of the periodic table are a mixed bag. Some of the elements are metals, though they barely act like metals in chemical reactions and are often called **poor metals**. Other elements within these groups are definitely nonmetals, whereas still other elements—metalloids—have a combination of metal and nonmetal features. Metals, metalloids, and nonmetals are sometimes even found in the same group. Scientists find it difficult to agree on one name for all these groups, so many researchers just call them the **BCNOs**, after the first element in each group (Boron, Carbon, Nitrogen, and Oxygen).

The BCNOs contain elements that are very important to life on Earth, such as oxygen, carbon, and nitrogen. They also include metals that were useful to early civilizations and metalloids that make up the computer chips and high-tech devices of today.

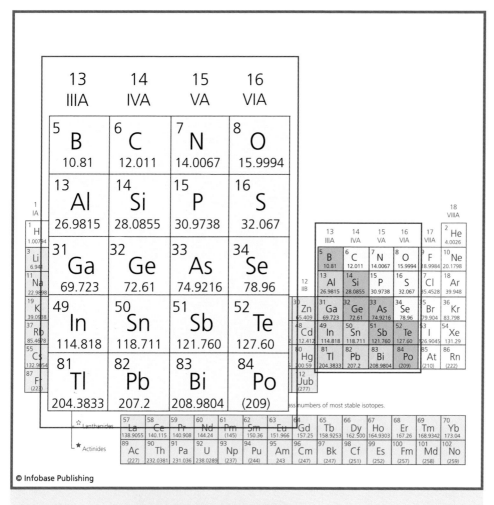

Figure 7.1   Groups 13 to 16 of the periodic table.

As might be expected from their position in the periodic table, elements in the four groups are in a transition zone between true metals and stable gases. To the left of the BCNOs in the table, the true metals tend to give up electrons in their mostly empty valence shells to other atoms. To the right of the BCNOs in the table, gases with mostly full valence shells seize or share electrons with other atoms. BCNOs, depending on whether they act more like a metal or nonmetal, may be involved in both kinds of electron activity, since they have valence shells that are about half full.

The poor metals among the BCNOs usually include aluminum, gallium, indium, thallium, tin, lead, and bismuth. The metalloids are boron, silicon, germanium, arsenic, antimony, tellurium, and polonium. The nonmetals are carbon, nitrogen, oxygen, phosphorus, sulfur and selenium. These groups are not "official," and chemists sometimes disagree on whether a particular element like boron should be called a metal or a metalloid.

The BCNOs, along with the halogens of Group 17 and the noble gases of Group 18, are part of the periodic table's *p* **block**. The *p* block is named after the fact that electrons involved in chemical reactions in these elements come from the *p* orbital.

It may not seem like a gas such as nitrogen has anything in common with a heavy metal such as lead. But the BCNOs share an important feature: their ability to make many different chemical partnerships. The "in-between" behavior of BCNO elements— whether it acts like a metal, a nonmetal or a little of both—makes it easy for them to team up with a wide variety of elements.

COMPOUNDS FOR LIFE

Without partnerships between some of the BCNO nonmetals, there would be no life on Earth. All plants and animals need oxygen in every one of their cells to survive. Oxygen combines with nearly every other element, even some of the gases in Group 18 that do not usually combine with anything else. Carbon atoms bind together in strong chains in DNA **molecules** and numerous other compounds in cells, including **carbohydrates** such as the sugars that provide fuel for cells.

An isotope of carbon called *carbon-14* offers a glimpse of how humans may have lived thousands of years ago. The radioactive isotope decays steadily to become nitrogen-14 in a way that is similar to the decay of potassium into argon, making it useful for dating plants, bones, and other **organic** materials that once contained carbon from archaeological sites. The half-life of carbon-14 is about 5,730 years. One of the most famous recent cases of carbon-14 dating is the "Iceman," the mummified body of a man found frozen high in the mountains between Italy and Austria. Carbon-14 dating of the body and of his well preserved clothing, tools, and

THE MAJOR ELEMENTS IN YOUR BODY

Several of the BCNO elements are necessary for life on Earth, so it makes sense that they also make up a large part of the human body. For instance, oxygen makes up 61% of the total body weight of an average human. Carbon, nitrogen, phosphorus, and sulfur are also ranked among the top 10 elements that contribute to body weight. Other top 10 elements—including calcium, potassium, sodium, chlorine, and hydrogen—form important compounds with the top BCNO elements in bone, heart muscle, and brain tissue.

Fourteen other elements show up in such tiny traces in the body that they are usually measured in parts per million, or about the size of a single drop in 13 gallons (49.2 liters) of water. These elements are mostly metals like magnesium and iron, but they do include less common elements such as cobalt and vanadium.

The human body also absorbs certain elements such as gold and aluminum from food, water, and air that are not useful but are also not dangerous in such tiny amounts. When the body absorbs more toxic elements such as uranium, lead, and cadmium, however, tiny amounts stored in the bones and liver can cause serious harm.

even the remains of his last meal inside his body show that he lived almost 5,500 years ago.

Phosphorus combined with oxygen makes up much of our bones and teeth. Phosphorus is also found in the molecule ATP, which delivers chemical energy inside cells. These two roles for phosphorus, especially the part it plays in creating ATP, make the element essential for human life. But some compounds of oxygen and phosphorus called *organophosphates* can be deadly. Organophosphates are the key ingredient in powerful insect killers such as diazinon and malathion, and can cause serious nerve damage in humans. Organophosphates are also found in deadly nerve gases such as sarin, which killed 12 people in a terrorist attack on a subway in Japan in 1995 and as many as 5,000 people in the 1988 Halabja poison gas attack by the Iraqi government.

Nitrogen gas, which makes up 78% of the Earth's air, is another BCNO element that is necessary for life but also has a destructive side. Nitrogen combines with oxygen to deliver chemical messages inside cells. Nitrogen also joins carbon as an important part of DNA molecules. The element, however, is also an important part of photochemical **smog**, a type of air pollution created when sunlight reacts with several compounds, including nitrogen dioxide. Gunpowder, nitroglycerine (the main ingredient in dynamite), and the explosive TNT all contain nitrogen compounds that turn into violently expanding nitrogen gas when they are heated. (The Nobel Prizes, the world's most famous awards in science and writing, were named after Alfred Nobel, the Swedish inventor of dynamite.) Nitrogen gas is also behind the tiny but lifesaving explosion that inflates a car's air bag in a crash.

The BCNO elements also play an important part in how the Earth itself looks today. For instance, the oxygen gas ozone is part of a layer in the atmosphere that protects the planet from the Sun's damaging radiation. Plants constantly change carbon dioxide gas into the oxygen and food that keeps animals alive. Gasoline, oil, and coal are all **hydrocarbons**, the carbon compounds that humans depend on to fuel our cars and our homes. Bacteria and algae turn nitrogen into compounds such as ammonia fertilizer and other sources of energy for all living things.

PRODUCTIVE AND POISONOUS

Most BCNO elements show up in useful products as part of a compound. For instance, nitrogen combines with hydrogen to make ammonia. Ammonia itself combines with other elements to make cleaning liquid, fertilizer, and explosives, among other products. A compound of boron and oxygen melts only at high temperatures, so it is used in Pyrex® oven dishes. Silicone, a plastic compound made from silicon and oxygen, also holds together under high heat and is waterproof. Silicone is used in car engines, window seals, and even hair conditioner. A compound made with bismuth, the heaviest nonradioactive element, is the key ingredient in the medicine Pepto-Bismol® that protects the stomach against acid. Bismuth compounds also give a shiny appearance to eye shadow and lipstick.

Sulfur compounds are used to make rubber strong enough to be used in tires, in a process called **vulcanization**. Sulfur is also used to make detergent, paper, fertilizers, and medicines. Several sulfur compounds have a strong odor to them. Onions, garlic, skunk spray, and even bad breath get their unique odor from sulfur compounds. Sulfur by itself has no smell.

Aluminum, tin, and lead are all well-known elements with a long history of being combined with other metals. The discovery of bronze, an alloy of tin and copper, brought drastic changes to weapons and tools for ancient civilizations in about 3500 B.C. Today, tin is used in **solder**, an alloy that can be melted and used as a kind of glue to stick together other pieces of metal or electronic parts. Tin is also alloyed with copper and other metals to make pewter, a bright, silver-like metal that is mostly used in plates, mugs, and home decorations. Lightweight aluminum forms an alloy with

Figure 7.2   Sulfur is probably most famous for its foul stench. It distinguishes the odor of a skunk's scent and is used to create a multitude of everyday items, such as paper and detergent.

many other metals and is used in everything from soda cans to special metal foam used to soundproof rooms. Aluminum is also so highly **reflective** that it is used in solar mirrors that generate solar power and heat-reflecting blankets used in to keep people warm in medical emergencies or during surgery. Aluminum is also a popular metal because it costs less to recycle aluminum than to extract it from new ore.

Among the more unusual BCNO compounds is antimony oxide, which is used to fireproof toys, car seats, and airplane parts. The compound reacts with burning material to form a chemical layer that blankets and extinguishes the flame. In ancient times, the Egyptians mixed a compound of antimony and sulfur with fat to make kohl, a black cosmetic used to color eyebrows and line eyes with a dark ring. All living things seem to need a tiny bit of the

BCNO selenium in their cells, but the element is also very useful in machines such as photocopiers and light meters. Selenium metal conducts electricity much better when exposed to light, which

BEAUTY AND THE BUCKYBALL

The latest trend in lip gloss is tiny—about 100,000 times smaller than the width of a human hair. In skin creams, sunscreens and cosmetics, the hot new ingredients are nanoparticles. These extremely small molecules are about one-billionth of a meter in size. When molecules get this small, they act differently than larger or "normal"-sized molecules.

One of the most famous nanoparticles is the buckyball, a molecule made up of 60 carbon atoms arranged in a soccer-ball shape. Some skin creams now include buckyball molecules. Another widely used nanoparticle is zinc oxide. For years, swimmers applied zinc oxide as a thick sunscreen paste, but the new nano-sized version of the compound is so small that it looks transparent when slathered on as sunblock. The makers of these products say the nanoparticles can reflect light and fight off damage to skin cells better than normal-sized particles. A few cosmetics manufacturers are experimenting with nanoparticles in eye shadow and lipsticks to see if the tiny molecules can produce different colors or new visual effects like iridescence, where colors seem to constantly change.

Nanoparticles are now used in a number of everyday products, including stain-resistant clothing and socks woven with nano-silver particles that kill off bacteria and fungi and keep feet smelling fresh. Nanoparticles have become so popular that scientists and governments are starting to look more closely at whether these molecules could be dangerous to human health or to the environment.

Researchers recently discovered that the nano-beauty secret of the twenty-first century might be a new twist on a very old idea. A team of French scientists studied a recipe for hair dye used by ancient Egyptians more than 4,000 years ago, and discovered that the dye's black color comes from lead sulfide nanocrystals.

makes it ideal for these electronic devices. The BCNO semiconductor silicon, best known for its role in computers and electronics, shines in a different light in gemstones like opal and agate.

Lead is one BCNO that is less popular now than in the past. For centuries, lead compounds were used in water pipes and more

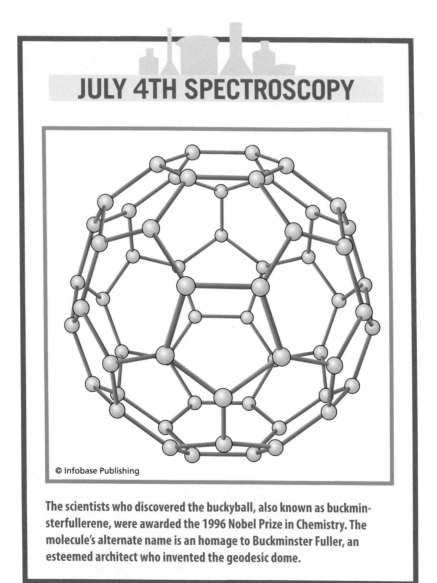

JULY 4TH SPECTROSCOPY

© Infobase Publishing

The scientists who discovered the buckyball, also known as buckminsterfullerene, were awarded the 1996 Nobel Prize in Chemistry. The molecule's alternate name is an homage to Buckminster Fuller, an esteemed architect who invented the geodesic dome.

recently used in paint and gasoline. Unfortunately, lead poisoning keeps the body from making new red blood cells and can eventually cause death if enough lead is absorbed by the body. The element is still found in a few products like batteries and the glass on computer and television screens, where its many electrons block the radiation coming out of these machines.

Lead is not the only silent killer among the BCNO elements. Arsenic, antimony, and thallium compounds have all been used as weed and insect killers and rat poisons. These elements can also poison the soil and water, so they are used more carefully and in smaller amounts than they were in the past century. All of these elements have also been used as slow murder weapons. They cause such ordinary problems—such as an upset stomach—that it can be

SUGAR OF LEAD

Up until the twentieth century, a white powdery chemical called *lead acetate* was a secret ingredient used to sweeten wine and preserve fruit. The Romans made a lead acetate syrup by boiling wine in lead pots. They then used it in other drinks and foods. The sweet wine may have been one reason that wealthy Romans often had gout, a painful disease of the joints that can be caused by high levels of lead in the blood. The practice of sweetening wine and other alcoholic drinks with lead acetate continued for centuries, even as people began to recognize that lead could be a poisonous element. Some researchers think that leaded wine may be behind the deaths of some famous people, including the composer Ludwig van Beethoven. Today, one of the main causes of lead poisoning comes from old paint chips, which small children may eat for their sweet taste.

hard to figure out if a person has been poisoned or died of a natural disease.

THE AGE OF SEMICONDUCTORS

Some important metalloids such as silicon and germanium are also called semiconductors. Semiconductors can conduct heat and electricity, although not as well as most metals, but they often act like nonconductors or **insulators**, too. Engineers can change the microscopic structure of a semiconductor by adding atoms of another element. Boron, phosphorus, gallium, and arsenic—all BCNOs—are the elements usually added to pure semiconductors, such as silicon and sometimes germanium. The additional atoms turn a semiconductor into a material in which the flow of electricity can be turned on and off and sent in different directions easily. Computer chips are made of thousands of semiconductors. At the most simple level, on-off switching and changes in electrical flow in the semiconductors are used by the chips to stand for "yes" and "no" answers to information carried electronically into the chip. Thousands of semiconductors working together in a chip are the brains behind computers, cellular phones, digital cameras, MP3 players, and similar electronic devices. Silicon can also transform sunlight into electricity, making it an important component of solar panels.

Silicon is the second most abundant element on Earth, after oxygen, but it is strangely missing from bacteria and animals. Carbon, silicon's close neighbor in the periodic table, became the most important element of life instead. Silicon may yet have its day, however. Computer technology has become so widespread and important to humans that some scientists say silicon is the new building block for the next generations of life on Earth.

SUMMARY

The BCNO elements are found in Groups 13 through 16 of the periodic table. The BCNO groups are a mixture of poor metals,

Figure 7.3 A scientist holds a very small silicon chip. Silicon, a semiconductor, has proven instrumental in numerous technological advances.

metalloids, and nonmetals. They include many of the elements essential for life on Earth, such as oxygen and carbon. They also include some important industrial metals such as aluminum and semiconductors such as silicon that are essential to computers and other high-tech machines.

Halogens and Noble Gases

Groups 17 and 18 of the periodic table are neighbors with little in common. Group 17 elements, called **halogens**, are among the most chemically reactive elements along with the alkali metals of Group 1. Group 18 elements, the **noble gases**, are the least reactive. In fact, the noble gases were named for their "royal" way of staying apart from other elements, like a king who lives in his palace far away from ordinary people. A few noble gases do not interact with any other elements at all.

The halogens are all poisonous nonmetals, but they are so reactive that they are rarely found alone in nature. Why do they pair up with other elements so easily and often? The clue, once again, is in their periodic table position. As Group 17 elements, their valence electron shell has seven electrons—only one electron away from being a full or complete shell. Many elements have an electron they can spare or at least share to fill a halogen's outer shell. Halogens have

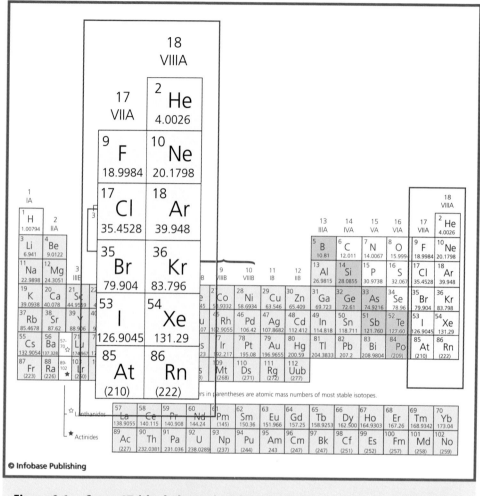

Figure 8.1   Group 17 (the halogens) and Group 18 (the noble gases) of the periodic table.

a natural partner in the alkali metals because the alkali metals do best in chemical reactions where they can give away the lone electron in their outermost shell. The word halogen means "salt maker," since alkali metals and halogens combine to create several different salts.

Mendeleyev did not know about the noble gases when he wrote down his first periodic table. The noble gases were "hidden" from the experiments of chemists because they did not react with any other elements. In the late nineteenth century, chemists in England discovered most of the noble gases by figuring out a way to separate them from air. As their location in the periodic table shows, the noble gases have a full valence electron shell. With no need to gain or lose electrons, the gases rarely interact with other elements. Helium and neon have never been found in any compound. Chemists can make argon, krypton, and xenon react with other elements under special conditions in the laboratory.

The halogens and noble gases, along with the BCNOs in Groups 13 through 16 are part of the periodic table's *p* block. The *p* block is named after the fact that the valence electrons in these elements come from the *p* orbital.

HARNESSING THE HALOGENS

The high reactivity of halogens is a double-edged sword for humans. Since halogens are eager to bond with so many elements, they have inspired a little bit of "mad scientist" creativity among chemists and others. Fluorine and chlorine, the two halogen gases, are especially good partners in compounds used to create new materials and transform other materials.

Toothpaste is one of the first things that come to mind when people hear about fluorine. The compound sodium fluoride is the most popular toothpaste additive. Fluoride changes tooth enamel into a harder form that protects the teeth from the acids that decay them. Fluorocarbons, a combination of fluorine and short chains of carbon atoms, are the material behind nonstick Teflon® and Gore-Tex® waterproof clothing. Fluorine is the main ingredient in some antifungal and antibiotic medicines and is among the chemicals used in general anesthesia before surgery. The highly active gas is also used to scratch tiny circuits in the silicon computer chips.

Chlorine is probably familiar to most people as part of household bleach or the chemical used to keep swimming pools clean. Chlorine compounds are used to kill germs, manufacture

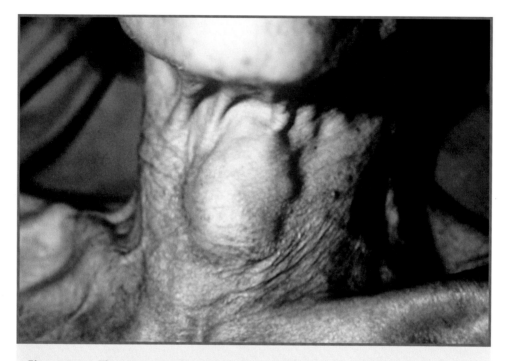

Figure 8.2   The person in this photograph suffers from a swelling of the thyroid gland. Iodine is responsible for regulating the health of this gland.

medicines, and sometimes bleach paper. Polyvinyl chloride or PVC plastic is found in everything from pipes to lawn chairs to floors. Chlorine gas was first used as a weapon in World War I by the Germans on Allied troops at the Second Battle of Ypres. The heavy, greenish yellow gas settled into the soldiers' trenches and caused thousands of them to stop breathing and die.

Astatine, the heaviest halogen, is so highly radioactive that less than a gram of it has ever existed on Earth. Bromine and iodine are slightly less reactive than fluorine and chlorine and have fewer uses. Camera film uses a light-sensitive compound of bromine and silver, and bromine produces a rich purple dye. Before lead was recognized as a toxic pollutant and removed from gasoline, bromine was added to gas as a way to prevent engine "knocking," the shuddering caused by gas burning unevenly in the engine. The manufacturers of citrus-flavored sodas and drinks add a mix of vegetable oil and bromine to their products to keep the citrus flavors mixed throughout the liquid.

Iodine is a germ-killer like chlorine and is also necessary for the health of the thyroid gland in humans. In fact, people who live close to nuclear power plants are often given emergency supplies of potassium iodine pills, in case the power plant has a leak of radioactive iodine. The pills flood the thyroid with normal iodine to keep the gland from absorbing the more harmful radioactive version of the element.

Some halogen compounds have been too reactive for the health of people and the planet. They can destroy healthy cells and attack the Earth's atmosphere in the same active way that they kill germs or break down wood into paper. For instance, chlorofluorocarbon or CFC compounds used to be popular cooling chemicals in refrigerators and air conditioners and in the gas that pushed hairspray and deodorant out of aerosol cans. CFCs are now widely banned because they destroy Earth's atmosphere. Chlorine is also part of the insect killer DDT, a dry cleaning fluid, and the compounds called PCBs. All of these products are now banned or used rarely because they have been linked to pollution and health problems like cancer and liver disease.

THE BRIGHT LIGHTS OF GROUP 18

Almost everyone has seen the brilliant and burning red color of a neon sign. But neon, along with the other noble gases, is naturally colorless and has no smell or taste. Neon red—along with helium peach, argon violet, krypton green, and xenon blue—comes from a special electric nudge.

Neon lights up when an electric charge travels through the gas as it sits inside a glass tube or other enclosed container. Electrons in the neon atoms absorb this incoming electric charge. The charge's energy acts like a shove that pushes electrons from their normal energy shells into shells that are at a higher energy level. The electrons fall back into their normal shells to keep the atom stable by releasing the electric energy as a particle of light. These particles give neon and other noble gases their special glow.

Lights are what noble gases do best. Along with the colored lights they produce, noble gases also fill regular light bulbs. The tungsten filament inside light bulbs breaks down when it is exposed to the oxygen in normal air. As a solution, light bulb makers sometimes surround the delicate wire with a noble gas like argon,

OZONE EATERS

About 12 to 15 miles (about 20 to 25 km) above the Earth's surface, a thin blanket of gas protects us from the Sun's harmful rays. The blanket is ozone, triplets of oxygen atoms bound together in molecules that absorb the Sun's ultraviolet radiation. In the 1970s, scientists discovered that the ozone layer was under attack from CFCs.

CFCs released from a can of hairspray do not just disappear, the researchers found. They float up high into the ozone layer, where they are broken apart by ultraviolet radiation. The wreckage of a CFC molecule contains highly active chlorine atoms that can destroy ozone.

In the 1980s, scientists studying the atmosphere over Antarctica shocked the world by announcing they had found a "hole" in the ozone layer over that continent. The startling discovery led to an international treaty called the Montreal Protocol that banned the use of CFCs in most products. Nearly all of the world's countries have signed the treaty, leading to a sharp decrease in the amount of ozone-eating CFCs in the atmosphere.

which does not react at all with the tungsten. Krypton and xenon are used in camera flashes and the lights that line airport runways. The intense but short-lived flashes of white light produced by xenon flash lamps are also used as strobe lights, like those found in dance clubs. The light of helium-neon lasers is used in the checkout scanners at grocery stores.

Most of the other uses for noble gases take advantage of their stable and nonreactive form. Silicon chips for computers are sometimes manufactured in a helium atmosphere because they can be

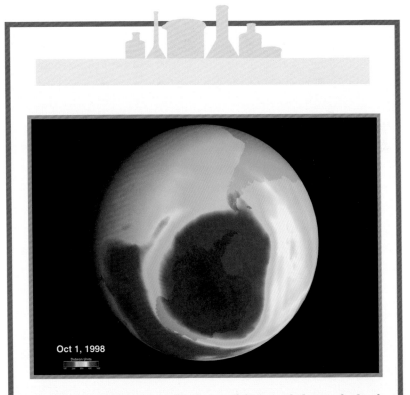

Oct 1, 1998

Dobson Units

An October 1, 1998, NASA satellite image of the ozone hole over the South Pole. The hole was alarmingly large, most likely due to an overabundance of CFCs in the atmosphere that break apart the oxygen molecules of the ozone layer.

assembled cleanly without interacting with destructive oxygen molecules in the air. Argon also offers a nonreactive environment for making steel, and it is pumped into the top of wine barrels to keep the oxygen in air from reacting with the wine. For similar reasons, museum exhibits such as paintings and old documents like the Declaration of Independence are sometimes encased in protective argon-filled containers. After the fiery 1937 crash of the *Hindenburg*, which was filled with highly reactive hydrogen gas, balloons and blimps are filled instead with lightweight and nonreactive helium.

Helium, the lightest noble gas and probably the second element ever formed in the universe, has several other interesting uses. The element freezes at very low temperatures, close to −430°F (about −257°C), which makes it very useful for cooling other materials. For instance, liquid helium is used to cool the very strong magnets used in magnetic resonance imaging, or MRI. (Doctors use MRI machines to see bones and soft tissues inside the body in more detail than can be seen with a simple X-ray.) Helium is also mixed with oxygen in the air tanks of deep-sea divers. Deep below the ocean's surface, the oxygen and nitrogen in air become more easily dissolved into the bloodstream. The extra nitrogen in the blood can make divers feel disoriented and sometimes cause "the bends," a painful condition where nitrogen bubbles form in the blood. Too much dissolved oxygen in the blood can eventually poison the brain. Divers have less chance of these life-threatening problems when they carry a mix of oxygen and helium, which is much harder to dissolve in the bloodstream.

Like the heavy elements of other groups, the noble gases have their own very radioactive member in radon. Radon can break down into dangerous isotopes that find their way into the lungs and cause cancer. In fact, radon is the second largest cause of lung cancer in the United States after cigarette smoke. In the 1980s, scientists discovered that dangerous radon could build up in basements and ground-floor rooms in houses that did not have enough windows or other places for the gas to escape. Radon also collects in underground mines.

SUMMARY

The halogens are found in Group 17 of the periodic table. The noble gases are found in Group 18. The halogens are highly reactive, most often forming compounds with alkali metals in Group 1. The noble gases are mostly nonreactive. The halogens have some important industrial roles but have also proved poisonous to humans and the environment in several cases. The noble gases are known for their distinctive colors when charged with electricity.

At the Table's Edge

From the time that they first used tools and tried to change their environment in other ways, humans have known that the world is made up of basic materials. Thousands of years later, ancient civilizations agreed on a few main elements such as fire and water that they thought were the building blocks of everything on Earth. The modern list of elements and their properties was discovered only in the past few hundred years. The simple yet elegant family tree of all matter, the periodic table of the elements, was finally uncovered in the nineteenth century. The building blocks of elements themselves—the reason that the periodic table is periodic—were not known until the early twentieth century, when subatomic particles were finally revealed. The most recent elements added to the periodic table did not exist at all until scientists identified them in the debris of war and created them from scratch in the middle of the twentieth century.

But is the long history of the periodic table of elements finally over? After all, the boxes have been filled, and the pattern that connects them into periods and groups is well known. Are scientists and inventors, doctors and artists still interested in the periodic table and the things it can tell us?

The answer is a definite "yes." Ever since Mendeleyev transformed a simple list of elements into a useful scientific tool, the periodic table has been the doorway through which researchers of all kinds can explore the universe of matter. Old elements are put to new uses, like the zinc nanoparticles in sunscreen. Familiar reactions are found to create serious problems, such as the destruction of the ozone layer by chlorofluorocarbons. Like Mendeleyev himself, scientists are predicting the existence of brand-new elements that have never been seen but are certain to be built someday in the laboratory.

The future of chemistry still lies within the rows and columns of the periodic table, as some cutting-edge research proves. The future of life also lies within the periodic table as people are constantly looking for ways to improve the quality of life through medicines, alternative fuels, and high-tech gadgets.

LOOKING FOR SPACE CREATURES ON EARTH

If life is discovered elsewhere in the universe, will it look like life on Earth? Scientists are preparing themselves for the first glimpse of extraterrestrial life by looking at some of the most bizarre and otherworldly creatures that live on this planet. They study **extremophiles**, bacteria and other animals such as tube worms, that live in the midst of harsh chemicals or very hot and cold temperatures. These animals live in places that most living things avoid, such as the frozen soil of Antarctica, cracks in the sea floor filled with scalding hot water, or the chemical soup of a hot mineral spring. Instead of depending on oxygen for their survival, many extremophiles rely instead on sulfur, a closely related BCNO element. If life does exist on other planets that do not have Earth's unusual oxygen-filled atmosphere, it might look and act like sulfur-loving bacteria, researchers suggest.

THE BIRTH OF A "SUPERATOM"

In 1995, two scientists in Colorado found a way to chill rubidium atoms to less than one-millionth of a degree above absolute zero, the coldest possible temperature. At this shockingly low temperature, the atoms did something that had never been seen before. They turned into an entirely new state of matter, called a **Bose-Einstein condensate** or BEC. In a BEC, the very cold temperatures force each atom in a group of atoms into exactly the same energy level. When this happens, each individual atom cannot be separated from the rest and all the atoms collapse into one "superatom" or BEC. Since 1995, other scientists have made superatoms from sodium, hydrogen, helium, potassium, ytterbium, cesium, and chromium atoms. Researchers are still not sure how Bose-Einstein condensates might be used. Some ideas include using the superatoms as parts of tiny, molecule-sized computers or as BEC beams that work like lasers.

MEDICAL METALS

Today's medical researchers are finding out that ancient alchemists may have been on to something when they mixed up different metals to cure certain illnesses. Scientists have known for a long time that metals like copper and zinc are important to human health. But studies now show that tiny amounts of many other metals are necessary for cells in the body to do their work—metals such as selenium, arsenic, and molybdenum that can be toxic at high doses. Scientists now combine what they know about the biology of cells with information about the atomic structure and reactions of metal elements to invent new drugs. For instance, vanadium is now used in medicines to treat diabetes. Patients with kidney failure take lanthanum carbonate, a compound of lanthanum, carbon, and oxygen, to fight dangerously high levels of phosphate in the blood.

Small amounts of gadolinium and indium make MRI pictures of the body clearer and easier for doctors to read.

MEMORY IN A FLASH

Cell phones, digital cameras, MP3 players, and memory sticks for computers all depend on a device called flash memory. Flash memory is a way to store information in all kinds of electronic gadgets even when they are unplugged or not receiving power from another source like a battery. In a little over a decade, flash memory has become such a large part of modern electronics that researchers are already looking for ways to improve it. Flash memory devices are built out of silicon, but many scientists are now turning to other BCNO elements to make memory devices that work faster and hold more information. For instance, some researchers have built a new kind of flash memory out of carbon nanotubes, long, wire-like versions of the buckyball. A nanotube memory device would be hundreds of times smaller than today's flash devices. Three technology companies announced recently that they had developed a new alloy of germanium and antimony that could be used to make a memory device that works at least 500 times faster than flash memory. Another team of scientists is hoping to build a faster-than-flash memory device with an unusual ingredient— chunks of a living virus that normally infects tobacco plants. When these virus chunks are coated with nanoparticles of platinum, they can be used as tiny electrical switches that move from off to on in microseconds.

ELEMENTS AND ENDANGERED SPECIES

The rhinoceros is among the most endangered animals on Earth, yet many are still killed each year for their horns that can be sold for a high price to make knife handles and powdered medicine. Other endangered animals such as the burrowing owl are not hunted by humans but are still disappearing at an alarming rate. Scientists are now using tiny amounts of certain elemental isotopes to help track and protect these species. They have discovered that the hair, feathers, bone, and horns of animals like the rhino contain unique sets of isotopes. These isotopes find their way into animals mostly through the food they eat, adding up to a sort of chemical "fingerprint" that can tell a researcher exactly where an animal lived. For instance, scientists recently showed that rhinos living at a certain animal reserve in South Africa with strontium-rich volcanic rocks have a special strontium isotope in their horns. Endangered species detectives could use this strontium fingerprint in rhino horns that are sold around the world to figure out if the rhinos on the preserve are being hunted illegally for their horn. Other isotopes of hydrogen, carbon, nitrogen, and sulfur are used to track disappearing species from elephants to butterflies.

SUMMARY

These reports from the "edge" of elements research show that the story of the universe's building blocks is far from finished. More than 130 years after Mendeleyev discovered the pattern of the periodic table, people are still searching through the table to find new things to build, new problems to solve, and new ways to look at the world.

PERIODIC TABLE OF THE ELEMENTS

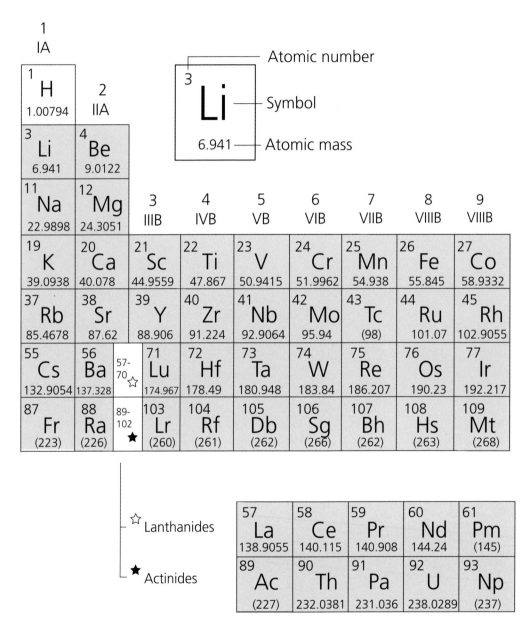

Numbers in parentheses are atomic mass numbers of most stable isotopes.

Metals

Non-metals

Metalloids

			13 IIIA	14 IVA	15 VA	16 VIA	17 VIIA	18 VIIA
								2 He 4.0026
			5 B 10.81	6 C 12.011	7 N 14.0067	8 O 15.9994	9 F 18.9984	10 Ne 20.1798
10 VIIIB	11 IB	12 IIB	13 Al 26.9815	14 Si 28.0855	15 P 30.9738	16 S 32.067	17 Cl 35.4528	18 Ar 39.948
28 Ni 58.6934	29 Cu 63.546	30 Zn 65.409	31 Ga 69.723	32 Ge 72.61	33 As 74.9216	34 Se 78.96	35 Br 79.904	36 Kr 83.798
46 Pd 106.42	47 Ag 107.8682	48 Cd 112.412	49 In 114.818	50 Sn 118.711	51 Sb 121.760	52 Te 127.60	53 I 126.9045	54 Xe 131.29
78 Pt 195.08	79 Au 196.9655	80 Hg 200.59	81 Tl 204.3833	82 Pb 207.2	83 Bi 208.9804	84 Po (209)	85 At (210)	86 Rn (222)
110 Ds (271)	111 Rg (272)	112 Uub (277)						

62 Sm 150.36	63 Eu 151.966	64 Gd 157.25	65 Tb 158.9253	66 Dy 162.500	67 Ho 164.9303	68 Er 167.26	69 Tm 168.9342	70 Yb 173.04
94 Pu (244)	95 Am 243	96 Cm (247)	97 Bk (247)	98 Cf (251)	99 Es (252)	100 Fm (257)	101 Md (258)	102 No (259)

ELECTRON CONFIGURATIONS

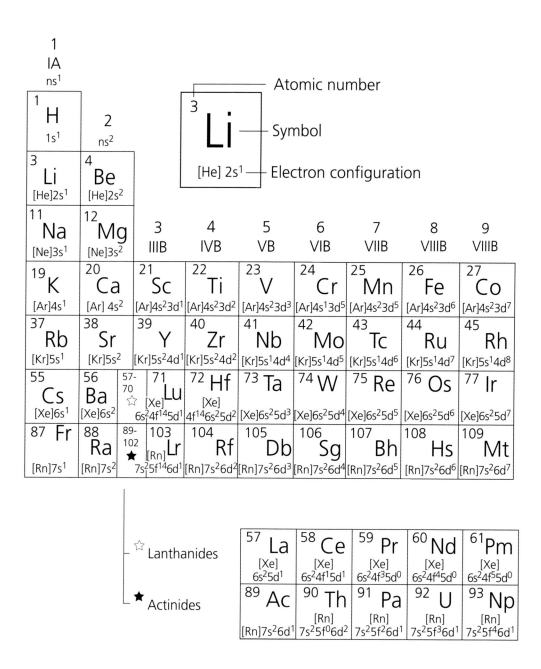

1 IA ns^1								
1 **H** $1s^1$	2 ns^2							
3 **Li** [He]$2s^1$	4 **Be** [He]$2s^2$							
11 **Na** [Ne]$3s^1$	12 **Mg** [Ne]$3s^2$	3 IIIB	4 IVB	5 VB	6 VIB	7 VIIB	8 VIIIB	9 VIIIB
19 **K** [Ar]$4s^1$	20 **Ca** [Ar] $4s^2$	21 **Sc** [Ar]$4s^23d^1$	22 **Ti** [Ar]$4s^23d^2$	23 **V** [Ar]$4s^23d^3$	24 **Cr** [Ar]$4s^13d^5$	25 **Mn** [Ar]$4s^23d^5$	26 **Fe** [Ar]$4s^23d^6$	27 **Co** [Ar]$4s^23d^7$
37 **Rb** [Kr]$5s^1$	38 **Sr** [Kr]$5s^2$	39 **Y** [Kr]$5s^24d^1$	40 **Zr** [Kr]$5s^24d^2$	41 **Nb** [Kr]$5s^14d^4$	42 **Mo** [Kr]$5s^14d^5$	43 **Tc** [Kr]$5s^14d^6$	44 **Ru** [Kr]$5s^14d^7$	45 **Rh** [Kr]$5s^14d^8$
55 **Cs** [Xe]$6s^1$	56 **Ba** [Xe]$6s^2$	57-70 ☆	71 **Lu** [Xe] $6s^24f^{14}5d^1$	72 **Hf** [Xe] $4f^{14}6s^25d^2$	73 **Ta** [Xe]$6s^25d^3$	74 **W** [Xe]$6s^25d^4$	75 **Re** [Xe]$6s^25d^5$	76 **Os** [Xe]$6s^25d^6$
87 **Fr** [Rn]$7s^1$	88 **Ra** [Rn]$7s^2$	89-102 ★	103 **Lr** [Rn] $7s^25f^{14}6d^1$	104 **Rf** [Rn]$7s^26d^2$	105 **Db** [Rn]$7s^26d^3$	106 **Sg** [Rn]$7s^26d^4$	107 **Bh** [Rn]$7s^26d^5$	108 **Hs** [Rn]$7s^26d^6$

(77 **Ir** [Xe]$6s^25d^7$; 109 **Mt** [Rn]$7s^26d^7$)

Atomic number
3 **Li**
Symbol
[He] $2s^1$ — Electron configuration

☆ Lanthanides

★ Actinides

57 **La** [Xe] $6s^25d^1$	58 **Ce** [Xe] $6s^24f^15d^1$	59 **Pr** [Xe] $6s^24f^35d^0$	60 **Nd** [Xe] $6s^24f^45d^0$	61 **Pm** [Xe] $6s^24f^55d^0$
89 **Ac** [Rn]$7s^26d^1$	90 **Th** [Rn] $7s^25f^06d^2$	91 **Pa** [Rn] $7s^25f^26d^1$	92 **U** [Rn] $7s^25f^36d^1$	93 **Np** [Rn] $7s^25f^46d^1$

								18 VIIIA ns^2np^6
		13 IIIA ns^2np^1	14 IVA ns^2np^2	15 VA ns^2np^3	16 VIA ns^2np^4	17 VIIA ns^2np^5		2 He $1s^2$

10 VIIIB	11 IB	12 IIB						
			5 B $[He]2s^22p^1$	6 C $[He]2s^22p^2$	7 N $[He]2s^22p^3$	8 O $[He]2s^22p^4$	9 F $[He]2s^22p^5$	10 Ne $[He]2s^22p^6$
			13 Al $[Ne]3s^23p^1$	14 Si $[Ne]3s^23p^2$	15 P $[Ne]3s^23p^3$	16 S $[Ne]3s^23p^4$	17 Cl $[Ne]3s^23p^5$	18 Ar $[Ne]3s^23p^6$
28 Ni $[Ar]4s^23d^8$	29 Cu $[Ar]4s^13d^{10}$	30 Zn $[Ar]4s^23d^{10}$	31 Ga $[Ar]4s^24p^1$	32 Ge $[Ar]4s^24p^2$	33 As $[Ar]4s^24p^3$	34 Se $[Ar]4s^24p^4$	35 Br $[Ar]4s^24p^5$	36 Kr $[Ar]4s^24p^6$
46 Pd $[Kr]4d^{10}$	47 Ag $[Kr]5s^14d^{10}$	48 Cd $[Kr]5s^24d^{10}$	49 In $[Kr]5s^25p^1$	50 Sn $[Kr]5s^25p^2$	51 Sb $[Kr]5s^25p^3$	52 Te $[Kr]5s^25p^4$	53 I $[Kr]5s^25p^5$	54 Xe $[Kr]5s^25p^6$
78 Pt $[Xe]6s^15d^9$	79 Au $[Xe]6s^15d^{10}$	80 Hg $[Xe]6s^25d^{10}$	81 Tl $[Xe]6s^26p^1$	82 Pb $[Xe]6s^26p^2$	83 Bi $[Xe]6s^26p^3$	84 Po $[Xe]6s^26p^4$	85 At $[Xe]6s^26p^5$	86 Rn $[Xe]6s^26p^6$
110 Ds $[Rn]7s^16d^9$	111 Rg $[Rn]7s^16d^{10}$	112 Uub $[Rn]7s^26d^{10}$						

62 Sm [Xe] $6s^24f^65d^0$	63 Eu [Xe] $6s^24f^75d^0$	64 Gd [Xe] $6s^24f^75d^1$	65 Tb [Xe] $6s^24f^95d^0$	66 Dy [Xe] $6s^24f^{10}5d^0$	67 Ho [Xe] $6s^24f^{11}5d^0$	68 Er [Xe] $6s^24f^{12}5d^0$	69 Tm [Xe] $6s^24f^{13}5d^0$	70 Yb [Xe] $6s^24f^{14}5d^0$
94 Pu [Rn] $7s^25f^66d^0$	95 Am [Rn] $7s^25f^76d^0$	96 Cm [Rn] $7s^25f^76d^1$	97 Bk [Rn] $7s^25f^96d^0$	98 Cf [Rn] $7s^25f^{10}6d^0$	99 Es [Rn] $7s^25f^{11}6d^0$	100 Fm [Rn] $7s^25f^{12}6d^0$	101 Md [Rn] $7s^25f^{13}6d^0$	102 No [Rn] $7s^25f^{14}6d^1$

TABLE OF ATOMIC MASSES

ELEMENT	SYMBOL	ATOMIC NUMBER	ATOMIC MASS	ELEMENT	SYMBOL	ATOMIC NUMBER	ATOMIC MASS
Actinium	Ac	89	(227)	Francium	Fr	87	(223)
Aluminum	Al	13	26.9815	Gadolinium	Gd	64	157.25
Americium	Am	95	243	Gallium	Ga	31	69.723
Antimony	Sb	51	121.76	Germanium	Ge	32	72.61
Argon	Ar	18	39.948	Gold	Au	79	196.9655
Arsenic	As	33	74.9216	Hafnium	Hf	72	178.49
Astatine	At	85	(210)	Hassium	Hs	108	(263)
Barium	Ba	56	137.328	Helium	He	2	4.0026
Berkelium	Bk	97	(247)	Holmium	Ho	67	164.9303
Beryllium	Be	4	9.0122	Hydrogen	H	1	1.00794
Bismuth	Bi	83	208.9804	Indium	In	49	114.818
Bohrium	Bh	107	(262)	Iodine	I	53	126.9045
Boron	B	5	10.81	Iridium	Ir	77	192.217
Bromine	Br	35	79.904	Iron	Fe	26	55.845
Cadmium	Cd	48	112.412	Krypton	Kr	36	83.798
Calcium	Ca	20	40.078	Lanthanum	La	57	138.9055
Californium	Cf	98	(251)	Lawrencium	Lr	103	(260)
Carbon	C	6	12.011	Lead	Pb	82	207.2
Cerium	Ce	58	140.115	Lithium	Li	3	6.941
Cesium	Cs	55	132.9054	Lutetium	Lu	71	174.967
Chlorine	Cl	17	35.4528	Magnesium	Mg	12	24.3051
Chromium	Cr	24	51.9962	Manganese	Mn	25	54.938
Cobalt	Co	27	58.9332	Meitnerium	Mt	109	(268)
Copper	Cu	29	63.546	Mendelevium	Md	101	(258)
Curium	Cm	96	(247)	Mercury	Hg	80	200.59
Darmstadtium	Ds	110	(271)	Molybdenum	Mo	42	95.94
Dubnium	Db	105	(262)	Neodymium	Nd	60	144.24
Dysprosium	Dy	66	162.5	Neon	Ne	10	20.1798
Einsteinium	Es	99	(252)	Neptunium	Np	93	(237)
Erbium	Er	68	167.26	Nickel	Ni	28	58.6934
Europium	Eu	63	151.966	Niobium	Nb	41	92.9064
Fermium	Fm	100	(257)	Nitrogen	N	7	14.0067
Fluorine	F	9	18.9984	Nobelium	No	102	(259)

ELEMENT	SYMBOL	ATOMIC NUMBER	ATOMIC MASS	ELEMENT	SYMBOL	ATOMIC NUMBER	ATOMIC MASS
Osmium	Os	76	190.23	Silicon	Si	14	28.0855
Oxygen	O	8	15.9994	Silver	Ag	47	107.8682
Palladium	Pd	46	106.42	Sodium	Na	11	22.9898
Phosphorus	P	15	30.9738	Strontium	Sr	38	87.62
Platinum	Pt	78	195.08	Sulfur	S	16	32.067
Plutonium	Pu	94	(244)	Tantalum	Ta	73	180.948
Polonium	Po	84	(209)	Technetium	Tc	43	(98)
Potassium	K	19	39.0938	Tellurium	Te	52	127.6
Praseodymium	Pr	59	140.908	Terbium	Tb	65	158.9253
Promethium	Pm	61	(145)	Thallium	Tl	81	204.3833
Protactinium	Pa	91	231.036	Thorium	Th	90	232.0381
Radium	Ra	88	(226)	Thulium	Tm	69	168.9342
Radon	Rn	86	(222)	Tin	Sn	50	118.711
Rhenium	Re	75	186.207	Titanium	Ti	22	47.867
Rhodium	Rh	45	102.9055	Tungsten	W	74	183.84
Roentgenium	Rg	111	(272)	Ununbium	Uub	112	(277)
Rubidium	Rb	37	85.4678	Uranium	U	92	238.0289
Ruthenium	Ru	44	101.07	Vanadium	V	23	50.9415
Rutherfordium	Rf	104	(261)	Xenon	Xe	54	131.29
Samarium	Sm	62	150.36	Ytterbium	Yb	70	173.04
Scandium	Sc	21	44.9559	Yttrium	Y	39	88.906
Seaborgium	Sg	106	(266)	Zinc	Zn	30	65.409
Selenium	Se	34	78.96	Zirconium	Zr	40	91.224

GLOSSARY

Actinides   The elements from actinium (atomic number 89) to nobelium (atomic number 102).

Alchemy   A mixture of chemistry and philosophy practiced in the ancient world; its main goals were to transform metals into gold and find chemical potions that would cure disease and lengthen life.

Alkali metals   The elements found in Group 1 of the periodic table.

Alkaline earth metals   The elements found in Group 2 of the periodic table.

Alloy   A mixture of two or more metals or metals and nonmetals. An alloy has different properties than the metals or nonmetals by themselves.

Amalgam   An alloy of mercury with another metal or metals.

Atom   The smallest part of an element that still has all the properties of that element. An atom contains electrons and a nucleus of protons and neutrons.

Atomic number   The number of protons in an atom's nucleus.

Atomic weight   The weight of all the protons and neutrons found in the nucleus of an atom. The atomic mass written in an element's square on the periodic table is the average mass of all of an element's isotopes found in nature.

BCNO   The name given to the elements of Groups 13 through 16 of the periodic table. The names are from the first letters of the first elements in these groups: boron, carbon, nitrogen, and oxygen.

Bose-Einstein condensate   A state of matter, different from a solid, liquid or gas, formed when individual atoms cooled to temperatures close to absolute zero behave as a single large "superatom."

Buckyball   A very stable molecule of 60 carbon atoms arranged in a soccer-ball shape; often used in nanotechnology applications. The formal name for these molecules is buckminsterfullerene.

Capacitor   A device consisting of two conducting objects placed near each other that stores an electrical charge.

Carbohydrate   An organic compound such as a sugar or starch made of carbon, hydrogen, and oxygen that is a major energy source for animals.

Catalyst   Any matter that is used to change or speed up a chemical reaction without being changed itself or destroyed in the reaction.

Compound   Matter made of two or more elements joined together chemically. The resulting compound has different chemical properties than the elements themselves.

Conductor   An element or compound through which electricity or heat can flow freely.

Corrosion   The breakdown of a material, especially a metal, by chemical reaction. Rust, caused by a reaction of iron, water, and oxygen, is a common type of corrosion.

***d* block**   The section of the periodic table that includes the transition metal elements in Groups 3 through 12. The block is named after the *d* orbital that contains the elements' valence electrons.

Desiccant   A chemical that attracts water molecules and is used to dry out other materials.

DNA   A very long, large molecule that carries genetic information in all living things; also called deoxyribonucleic acid.

Electron   A tiny particle with a negative electrical charge that moves around the nucleus of an atom.

Electron shell   A space surrounding the nucleus of an atom where electrons travel; sometimes called an orbital or energy level.

Element   An atom of matter with a specific number of protons in its nucleus; the smallest building block of matter that cannot be broken down into two or more different kinds of matter.

Erosion   The process of wearing away soil, sand, or rock by the action of water, wind, or ice.

Extremophile   An animal, usually a single-celled bacterium, that lives in extreme conditions, such as very high or low temperatures, high or low air pressure, or high level of surrounding chemicals.

***f* block**   The section of the periodic table that includes the lanthanides and actinides. The block is named after the *f* orbital that contains the elements' valence electrons.

Fission   The process of splitting the nucleus of an atom into the nuclei of several lighter atoms, releasing a large amount of energy.

Fuel cell   A device that creates energy, usually electricity, by combining a fuel such as liquid hydrogen with oxygen.

Fusion   The process where nuclei of lighter atoms join together to create the nucleus of a heavier atom, releasing a large amount of energy.

Gas   A form of matter where particles move freely and can expand to fit any size and shape of its container.

Group   One of the 18 vertical columns in the periodic table. Elements in the same group usually, but not always, have similar properties.

Half-life   The time it takes for half of the atoms in a sample of radioactive material to break down, or decay.

Halogens   The elements found in Group 17 of the periodic table.

Hydrocarbon   Any kind of compound containing only hydrogen and carbon; the best-known hydrocarbons are fuels such as oil and gas.

Hypothesis   A temporary explanation for a scientific problem or observation that can be tested by further research.

Insulator   An element or compound through which electricity and heat do not flow freely.

Ion   An atom or group of atoms with extra or missing electrons. Extra electrons give the atoms a negative electrical charge, whereas missing electrons give the atoms a positive electrical charge.

Iridescence   A display of softly bright rainbow colors that may shift over time or depending on viewing light or viewing angle.

Island of stability   The name given to a possible group of transfermian elements where the number of protons and neutrons in the elements' nuclei are such that the nuclei are much more stable than other known transfermian elements.

Isotopes   Atoms of the same element that have different atomic weights due to different numbers of neutrons in the nucleus.

Lanthanides   The elements from lanthanum (atomic number 57) to lutetium (atomic number 70).

Liquid   A form of matter where particles move less freely than in a gas but more freely than in a solid; liquids can change their shape to fit any container but cannot expand to fill a container.

Mass   A measurement of an amount of matter. A measurement of mass is the same everywhere in the universe, where a measurement of weight is dependent on the pull of gravity.

Matter   Anything that has mass and takes up space, regardless of where in the universe it is located.

Metal   An element that easily conducts heat and electricity, has high boiling and melting temperatures, and tends to give up electrons in chemical reactions.

Metalloid   An element that has properties of both metals and nonmetals; sometimes called a *semiconductor*.

Misch metal   A manufactured mix of lanthanide elements and iron that easily produces sparks when struck or rubbed.

Molecule   A group of atoms joined by chemical bonds.

Nanoparticle   A particle of a single element or compound whose size is measured in nanometers, or one-billionth of a meter.

Neutron　A particle of matter with no electrical charge that binds to protons to make the nucleus of an atom.

Noble gases　The elements found in Group 18 of the periodic table.

Nonmetal　An element that does not easily conduct heat and electricity and tends to gain or share electrons in chemical reactions.

Nucleus　The center of an atom, made of protons and neutrons, which makes up most of an atom's mass.

Orbital　A path or energy level followed by an electron inside an electron shell.

Ore　A rock or mineral that contains metal that can be sold or traded.

Organic　Describes a chemical compound containing carbon; usually used to describe living things such as plants and animals.

Ozone　An unstable oxygen molecule consisting of three oxygen atoms; ozone collected in the Earth's atmosphere shields the planet from the Sun's ultraviolet light.

***p* block**　The section of the periodic table that includes the halogens and noble gases. The block is named after the *p* orbital that contains the elements' valence electrons.

Period　One of the seven horizontal rows in the periodic table. Periods track the addition of electrons to shells outside the nucleus of an atom.

Periodic　Happening or repeating after a specific amount of time or a specific amount of space.

Periodic table of the elements　An arrangement of all the elements by increasing atomic number in periods and groups that demonstrates their repeating nature.

Polarize　To alter the vibration of a light wave so that the direction of the wave changes from its original direction.

Poor metals   The metal-like elements of the BCNO groups; poor metals act like metals but are less reactive than the alkali and alkaline earth metals but more reactive than the transition metals.

Proton   A particle of matter with a positive electrical charge that binds to neutrons to make the nucleus of an atom.

Pyrotechnician   A specially trained expert who designs, manufactures, and explodes fireworks and flares.

Radioactivity   The energy released as the result of the breakdown or decay of the nucleus of an atom.

Reaction   A process of chemical change involving two or more elements or compounds; reactions can combine, exchange pieces between or break down the involved elements or compounds.

Refine   To bring to a pure state; to remove impure or additional materials.

Reflective   Bending or pushing back light from a surface.

s block   The section of the periodic table that includes the alkali and alkaline earth metals. The block is named after the *s* orbital that contains the elements' valence electrons.

Semiconductor   An element or compound that can conduct electricity better than an insulator (nonmetal) but not as well as a conductor (metal); the electrical flow in a semiconductor can be changed with a change in temperature or by adding other materials.

Smog   Air pollution caused by the reaction of sunlight and chemical compounds such as nitrogen dioxide and hydrocarbons; the compounds are usually produced by car exhaust and the release of gases from industries such as coal-fired power plants.

Solder   A metal alloy that can be melted to join together other metal pieces without melting the entire metal structure.

Solid   A form of matter where particles are held firmly in position. A solid has a definite mass and cannot change its shape to fit a container without breaking that shape.

Steel   A metal alloy that contains iron as its main ingredient along with some carbon and is hard, durable, and able to be shaped into different forms. Steel may contain a number of other elements including nickel, cobalt, manganese, and several other metals.

Superconductor   A material through which electricity flows freely, without any lost power.

Superheavy elements   *See* Transfermian elements.

Transfermian elements   The elements with atomic numbers higher than 100, the atomic number of fermium; sometimes called *superheavy elements.*

Transition metals   The elements of Groups 3 through 12 and Periods 4 through 7, excluding the lanthanides and actinides.

Transuranium elements   The elements with atomic numbers higher than 92, the atomic number of uranium.

Valence electron   An electron involved in a reaction between two or more elements. Valence electrons are usually, but not always, found in the outermost electron shell from an atom's nucleus.

Valence shell   The electron shell in which valence electrons are located.

Vapor   The gas form of a material normally found as a liquid or solid.

Vulcanization   A process where sulfur is added to natural rubber to make the rubber harder and more durable.

BIBLIOGRAPHY

Abbgy, Theodore S. *Elements and the Periodic Table: What Things Are Made Of.* Quincy, IL: Mark Twain Media, 2001.

Amin, Rajan, Max Bramer, and Richard Emslie. "Intelligent Data Analysis for Conservation: Experiments With Rhino Horn Fingerprint Identification." *Knowledge-Based Systems* 16 (2003): 329–336.

Atkins, P.W. *The Periodic Kingdom.* New York: BasicBooks, 1995.

Ball, Philip. *The Ingredients: A Guided Tour of the Elements.* Oxford, UK: University Press, 2002.

Boyce, Nell. "Safety of Nano-Cosmetics Questioned." "Morning Edition," National Public Radio Web site. Available online. URL: http://www.npr.org/templates/story/story.php?storyId=5257306.

Brown, Alan S. "Maglev Goes To Work." Mechanical Engineering Web site. Available online. URL: http://www.memagazine.org/june06/features/maglev/maglev.html.

Chang, Hao. "Chinese Terms for Chemical Elements: Characters Combining Radical and Phonetic Elements." *Chemistry International*, January-February 2004.

Emsley, John. *Nature's Building Blocks.* Oxford, UK: Oxford University Press, 2001.

Engber, Daniel. "Stay Out of That Balloon!: The Dangers of Helium Inhalation." Slate Web site. Available online. URL: http://www.slate.com/id/2143631.

Essick, Kristi. "Guns, Money and Cell Phones." *Industry Standard*, June 11, 2001.

Gordin, Michael D. *A Well-Ordered Thing: Dmitrii Mendeleev and the Shadow of the Periodic Table.* New York: BasicBooks, 2004.

Hofmann, Sigurd. *On Beyond Uranium: Journey to the End of the Periodic Table.* London: Taylor and Francis, 2002.

IBM. "Promising New Memory Chip Technology Demonstrated by IBM, Macronix and Qimonda Joint Research Team." IBM

Web site, press release. Available online. URL: http://www-03.ibm.com/press/us/en/pressrelease/20744.wss.

Knapp, Brian. *Elements, Compounds and Mixtures.* Danbury, CT: Grolier Education, 1998.

Koppenol, W.H. "Naming of New Elements: IUPAC Recommendations 2002." *Pure and Applied Chemistry* 74 (2002): 787–791.

Krebs, Robert E. *The History and Use of Our Earth's Chemical Elements.* Westport, CT: Greenwood Press, 1998.

Kurlansky, Mark. *Salt: A World History.* New York: Penguin Books, 2002.

Lu, X.B., and J.Y. Dai. "Memory Effects of Carbon Nanotubes as Charge Storage Nodes for Floating Gate Memory Applications." *Applied Physics Letters* 88 (2006): 113104.

Molina, Mario. J., and F. Sherwood Rowland. "Stratospheric Sink for Chlorofluoromethanes: Chlorine Atom-Catalysed Destruction of Ozone." *Nature* 249 (1974): 810–812.

Morris, Richard. *The Last Sorcerers.* Washington, DC: Joseph Henry Press, 2003.

NASA. "Exobiology: Life Through Space and Time." NASA Web site. Available online. URL: http://exobiology.nasa.gov/.

Neuzil, Mark, and William Kovarik. *Mass Media and Environmental Conflict: America's Green Crusades.* Thousand Oaks, CA: Sage Publications, 2005.

Redmond, Ian. "Coltan Boom, Gorilla Bust: The Impact of Coltan Mining on Gorillas and Other Wildlife in Eastern DR Congo." A Report for the Dian Fossey Gorilla Fund Europe and the Born Free Foundation, May 2001. Born Free Foundation Web site. Available online. URL: http://www.bornfree.org.uk/animals/gorillas/conservation-research/.

Reith, Frank, Stephen L. Rogers, D.C. McPhail, and Daryl Webb. "Biomineralization of Gold: Biofilms on Bacterioform Gold." *Science* 313 (2006): 233–236.

Scerri, Eric R. *The Periodic Table: Its Story and Its Significance.* New York: Oxford University Press, 2006.

Seaborg, Glenn. "Transuranium elements." Encyclopedia Britannica, Guide to the Nobel Prizes Web site. Available online. URL: http://www.britannica.com/nobel/macro/5001_20_326.html.

Seife, Charles. "Berkeley Crew Unbags Element 118." *Science* 293 (2001): 777–778.

Service, Robert F. "Berkeley Crew Bags Element 118." *Science* 284 (1999): 1751.

Slater, Jack. "Putting Soul into Science." *Ebony*, May 1973.

Thompson, Katherine H., and Chris Orbig. "Boon and Bane of Metal Ions in Medicine." *Science* 300 (2003): 936–939.

Tocci, Salvatore. *The Periodic Table.* New York: Children's Press, 2004.

Tseng, Ricky J., Tsai Chunglin, Ma Lipong, Ouyang Jianyong, Cengiz S. Ozkan, and Yang Yang. "Digital Memory Device Based on Tobacco Mosaic Virus Conjugated With Nanoparticles." *Nature Nanotechnology* 1 (2006): 72–77.

University of Colorado at Boulder Department of Physics. "BEC Homepage." Physics 2000 Web site. Available online. URL: http://www.colorado.edu/physics/2000/bec/index.html.

"Voyager Interstellar Mission." NASA Web site. Available online. URL: http://voyager.jpl.nasa.gov/spacecraft/goldenrec.html.

Walter, P., E. Welcomme, P. Hallégot, N.J. Zaluzec, C. Deeb, J. Castaing, P. Veyssière, R. Bréniaux, J. Lévêque, and G. Tsoucaris. "Early Use of PbS Nanotechnology for an Ancient Hair Dyeing Formula." *Nano Letters* 6 (2006): 2215–2219.

Weiss, R. "Study Concludes Beethoven Died From Lead Poisoning." *Washington Post*, December 6, 2005.

Wiker, Benjamin D. *The Mystery of the Periodic Table.* Bathgate, ND: Bethlehem Books, 2003.

FURTHER READING

Asimov, Isaac. *Building Blocks of the Universe*. London: Abelard-Schuman, 1974.

Atkins, P.W. *The Periodic Kingdom*. New York: BasicBooks, 1995.

Blobaum, Cindy. *The Periodic Table*. Austin, TX: Prufrock Press, 2005.

Cox, Roxbee. *Atoms and Molecules*. Tulsa, OK: EDC Publishers, 1993

Emsley, John. *Molecules at an Exhibition: Portraits of Intriguing Materials in Everyday Life*. New York: Oxford University Press, 1999.

Heiserman, David L. *Exploring Chemical Elements and Their Compounds*. New York: McGraw-Hill, 1991.

Nechaev, I., Gerald W. Jenkins, and Borin Van Loon. *The Chemical Elements: The Fascinating Story of Their Discovery and of the Famous Scientists Who Discovered Them*. St. Albans, UK: Tarquin Books, 1997.

Scerri, Eric R. *The Periodic Table: Its Story and Its Significance*. New York: Oxford University Press, 2006.

Stwertka, Albert. *A Guide to the Elements*. New York: Oxford University Press, 2002.

Tweed, Matt. *Essential Elements: Atoms, Quarks, and the Periodic Table*. New York: Walker and Company, 2003.

Zannos, Susan. *Dmitri Mendeleyev and the Periodic Table*. Hockessin, DE: Mitchell Lane Publishers, 2004.

Web Sites

Chemical Achievers: The Path to the Periodic Table

http://www.chemheritage.org/classroom/chemach/periodic/index.html

This site contains a short history of the scientists who made the discoveries leading up to Mendeleyev's modern periodic table.

ChemiCool: Periodic Table

http://www.chemicool.com

The ChemiCool table offers information about each element along with an easy-to-read chemistry dictionary.

It's Elemental: The Periodic Table

http://pubs.acs.org/cen/80th/elements.html

The magazine *Chemical and Engineering News* celebrated its eightieth birthday with these short essays and photos of each element in the periodic table.

The Origin of the Periodic Table

http://www.colorado.edu/physics/2000/periodic_table/index.html

Part of the University of Colorado's Physics 2000 project, this site explains the periodic table in a conversation between cartoon student "Alex Morales" and know-it-all scientist "Dr. Bob."

Periodic Table: Formulations

http://www.meta-synthesis.com/webbook/35_pt/pt.html

This site contains a wide selection of periodic tables throughout history, along with short explanations about their creators.

The Periodic Table of Comic Books

http://www.uky.edu/Projects/Chemcomics/

Each element in this unique periodic table is linked to comic books that mention the element. Click on "Co," for instance, and see the comic where the X-Men fought "Cobalt Man."

The Visual Elements Periodic Table

http://www.chemsoc.org/viselements/Pages/periodic_table.html

The Visual Elements table has a unique photograph, short Web videos and description for each element.

WebElements Periodic Table

http://www.webelements.com

This site is a good place to start looking at the periodic table and learning a little more about each element.

INDEX

PHOTO CREDITS

ABOUT THE AUTHOR

BECKY HAM received a B.A. in Anthropology from The University of Arizona and a Ph.D. in Biological Anthropology from New York University. She was a teaching assistant for anthropology and gross anatomy classes at New York University and has done archaeology and paleontology fieldwork in Arizona, Israel, and Tanzania. She is a science writer for the Center for the Advancement of Health and the American Association for the Advancement of Science. She has written articles on science and health topics for *Health* magazine, Discovery.com, and MSNBC.com, among other publications. She is a regular contributor to the American Chemical Society membership tabloid *Chemistry*.